DESKTOP PUBLISHING
IN

SANDRA L. BAREFIELD
BERRIEN SPRINGS HIGH SCHOOL
BERRIEN SPRINGS, MICHIGAN

DF22AB
PUBLISHED BY
SOUTH-WESTERN PUBLISHING CO.
CINCINNATI CARROLLTON, TX LIVERMORE, CA

Acquisitions Editor: Robert First
Developmental Editor: Dave Lafferty
Production Associate Editor: Joseph P. Powell III
Designer: Elaine Lagenaur
Photo Researcher: Donna Scenna

ISBN: 0-538-60707-6

Library of Congress Catalog Card Number: 89-64257

1 2 3 4 5 6 7 8 9 0 DH 9 8 7 6 5 4 3 2 1 0

Printed in the United States of America

PREFACE

DESKTOP PUBLISHING IN THE BAG contains a collection of independent, flexible exercises that provide supplementary practice materials to use while learning to operate your desktop publishing software. Use this book in conjunction with teacher instruction and your software manual. The numerous exercises provide an introduction to the field of desktop publishing. On completion of the exercises, you will have gained a working knowledge of how to design and create documents using desktop publishing software.

DESKTOP PUBLISHING IN THE BAG evokes a sports-related scenario that involves being a *player* on the *desktop publishing team* during the *Publishing Season*. The season opens with a review of what the season entails. Then *tryouts* are held to select players, a *training period* is conducted, and finally the actual *games* are played to conclude the Publishing Season. Because learning a desktop publishing skill follows the same developmental process as learning an athletic skill, the sports theme is both fun and appropriate!

DESKTOP PUBLISHING IN THE BAG is divided into four parts; each contains a variety of exercises. Part 1, *The Ground Rules*, defines desktop publishing, discusses the equipment used, and suggests the necessary background skills you should be familiar with before beginning the exercises.

Part 2, *The Game Fundamentals*, identifies the basic fundamentals (page setup, graphic files, graphic drawing tools, text, page assembly, and printing) used in operating desktop publishing software to design publications. The commands associated with each fundamental topic are explored through a series of simple tasks that stress individual concepts and develop a basic familiarity with operating DTP software.

Once an understanding of how to use the different features is established, Part 3, *The Practice Drills*, provides actual publications (letterheads, flyers, speciality items, and business forms) to be designed. Each type of publication includes a set of guidelines and individual practice drills containing strategies relating to page layout and design principles along with a possible design solution for the publication.

Part 4, *The Games*, challenges the students to put into practice their newly developed desktop publishing skills by designing several publications that are actually used in different businesses.

The materials presented in this text-workbook are generic and can be completed using most desktop publishing software. For example, you can elect to use Aldus' **Pagemaker®**,[1] Software Publishing's **First Publisher**,[2] Timeworks' **Publish It!™**,[3] or Springboard's **Publisher™**.[4] Your hardware and software capabilities will dictate how the exercises are completed.

---

[1]Pagemaker is a registered trademark of Aldus Corporation. Any reference to Pagemaker refers to this footnote.

[2]PFS:First Publisher is a registered trademark of Software Publishing Company. Any reference to PFS:First Publisher refers to this footnote.

[3]Publish It! is a trademark of Timeworks, Inc. Any reference to Publish It! refers to this footnote.

[4]Springboard Publisher is a trademark of Springboard Software, Inc. Any reference to Springboard Publisher refers to this footnote.

The suggested answers to the exercises were created using a Zenith® 286 computer,[5] Epson LX-86™ printer,[6] a Microsoft Mouse®,[7] Software Publishing Corporation's **PFS:® First Publisher** desktop publishing software, and South-Western's **CLIP ART FOLIO: A LIBRARY OF DESKTOP PUBLISHING ART** (Stock Number DF39AB).[8]

Your desktop publishing software may be capable of doing only some of the exercises in this book. If you have other software that works with your DTP software for the features that your DTP software does not have, then you can perform all the exercises. If you do not have other such software, you should skip the exercises you cannot perform.

---

[5]Zenith is a registered trademark and the Zenith 286 computer is a product of Zenith Data Systems.

[6]Epson LX-86 is a trademark of Epson America, Inc.

[7]Microsoft Mouse is a registered trademark of Microsoft Corporation.

[8]CLIP ART FOLIO: A LIBRARY OF DESKTOP PUBLISHING ART is a product of the South-Western Publishing Company.

CONTENTS

INTRODUCTION

PART 4
THE GAMES

Introduction

OBJECTIVES

1. To meet Clicker the Mouse.
2. To learn about the Publishing Season.
3. To review the parts of this book.
4. To learn how each part of the Publishing Season is organized.
5. To learn how to approach working through this book.

HELLO AND WELCOME!

You are about to begin an exciting adventure as you use DESKTOP PUBLISHING IN THE BAG. The *Publishing Season*, which provides an opportunity for you to participate in the so-called sport of *Desktop Publishing*, is ready to get under way. Those participating in the activities will be your instructor, better known as the *Coach*; you, the *Player*; and *Clicker the Mouse*, who will be the team manager.

Meet **Clicker the Mouse**. See Figure I.1. As you may know, or will soon find out, working with a computer to do desktop publishing can be

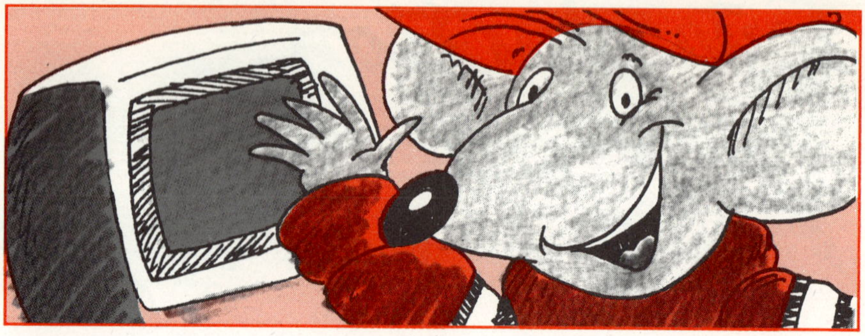

Figure I.1 Clicker the Mouse welcomes you to the Publishing Season!

rather frustrating at times. If something doesn't work, you need to try again. Clicker can help lighten your spirits as you proceed through this book.

As with any sport, it is necessary first to understand how the game is to be played. So read the following material carefully. It explains how you will progress through the Publishing Season.

AN OVERVIEW OF THE PUBLISHING SEASON

DESKTOP PUBLISHING IN THE BAG contains the items you will need as you go through the Publishing Season. If you have an outstanding season, it may even start you thinking about pursuing a professional career in the area of desktop publishing. But for now your goal is to make the DTP team and earn your *varsity letter* at the end of the Publishing Season. **DTP** stands for **D**esk**T**op **P**ublishing.

Therefore, before you try out for the team, you need to understand **The Ground Rules**, which provide information relating to the game itself, the equipment used, and the *playing field*. Then, to make the DTP team, you will learn the basic operating features of your desktop publishing software.

To accomplish this, you go through a series of *tryout sessions* in **The Game Fundamentals**, demonstrating your proficiency at performing each of the required tasks. Once you make the team, the work begins as you complete conditioning exercises called **The Practice Drills**. You will receive training on designing actual documents during this time. If you are successful at designing the publications, you will have the opportunity to play in the games.

During **The Games**, you design a series of publications for different businesses. This gives you a chance to become the star, since you will call all the signals. At the end of the season, the Coach decides who has earned a varsity DTP letter according to their season performance.

A REVIEW OF THE FOUR PARTS INCLUDED IN THE PUBLISHING SEASON

The following sections discuss the four different parts of this text-workbook. Familiarize yourself with the terminology for the Publishing Season.

Part 1—The Ground Rules (Provide an Orientation to DTP)

In *The Ground Rules*, you receive a brief introduction to the field of desktop publishing by learning about desktop publishing tasks and the types of equipment used to perform them. Then, since this text-workbook does not give directions relating to individual hardware configurations or specific software packages, you are directed to acquaint yourself with the pieces of equipment you will be using to perform the exercises. So double-check to be sure you have the following available to you before moving on to the next part:

- A microcomputer and printer (will determine what software can be used).
- A hardware manual (to refer to for specific instructions and answers to questions about hardware).
- Desktop publishing software (compatible with hardware; determines your limitations in completing the projects).
- Access to a software manual (for answering specific questions relating to your software).
- A data disk (to store the documents you design).

Part 2—The Game Fundamentals (Teach Basic Operating Features of DTP Software)

In *The Game Fundamentals*, you learn how to operate your DTP software and develop the foundation on which your skills will be built. The same routine is followed in completing each *tryout session* for the six basic fundamentals involved in doing desktop publishing—page setup, graphic files, graphic drawing tools, text, page assembly, and printing.

After the fundamentals are covered and you are familiar with operating your individual software, a *tryout session* addresses the first step in the DTP cycle: preplanning your document. Once you have completed this part, you are ready to move on to designing publications.

Use the following routine for each of the tryout sessions:

1. Read the explanation of the fundamental topic to be learned.
2. If you are unfamiliar with a term, refer to the list of definitions that explain the terminology used in that tryout session.
3. Review the list of goals identifying the steps you will perform during the tryout session.
4. Complete the actual tryout session where you are directed to perform specific tasks at the computer and record keystrokes and/or commands used in completing the task.

Part 3—The Practice Drills (Develop Design Techniques Used in DTP)

To strengthen your newly learned skills, you will design four types of publications—letterheads, flyers, speciality items, and business forms—in *The Practice Drills*. Prior to beginning the actual drills, read the guidelines that highlight general points to consider in relation to the type of publication being designed. Then, as you complete each practice drill, develop the habit of following the DTP cycle (planning, designing, assembling, and printing) so it becomes routine and happens naturally as you design publications.

You will want to pay close attention to the strategies that present suggestions relating to proven design principles. Remember, these are unwritten rules. There are no right or wrong ways to design publications; if it works for you, use it. Sometimes the most successful publications are those that break the rules.

Use the following steps for each of the practice drills. Note that the steps differ slightly for Drills A–C and Drill D.

Drill A (Letterheads), Drill B (Flyers), and Drill C (Speciality Items):

Each practice drill is presented using the format shown in Figure I.2. This format will indicate the *Practice Goal to Accomplish*, *Strategies to Consider*,

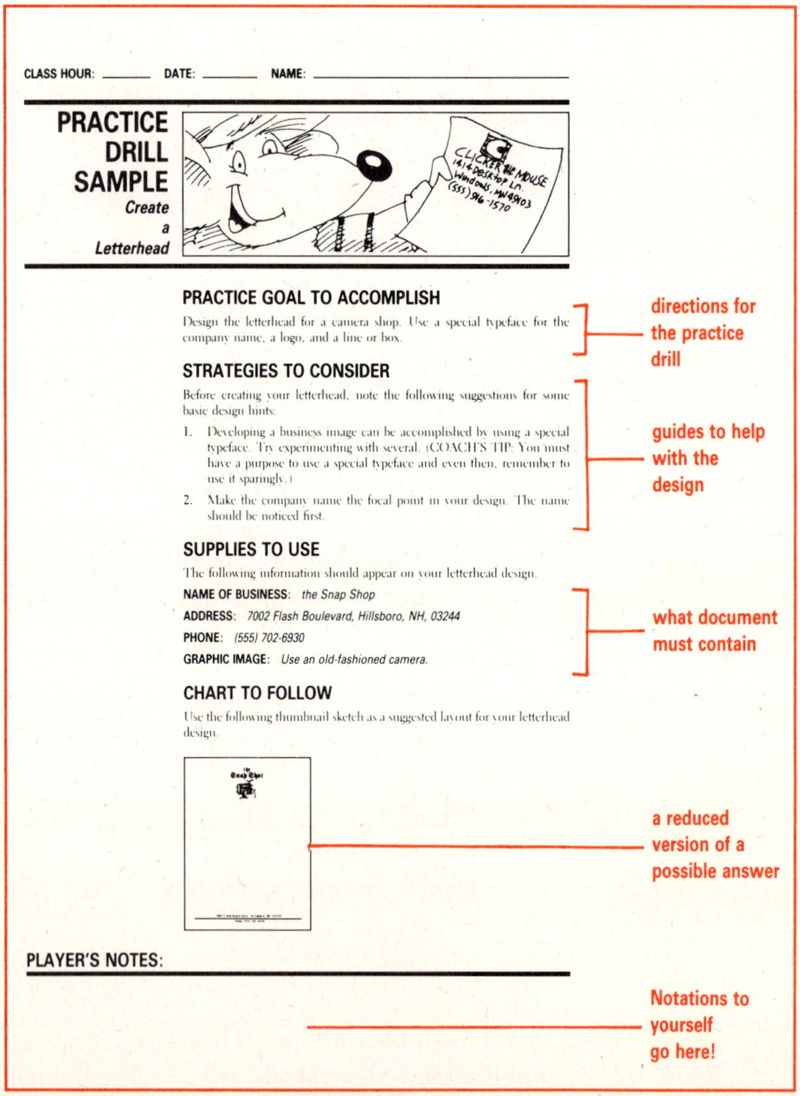

CLASS HOUR: ______ DATE: ______ NAME: ______________________

PRACTICE DRILL SAMPLE
Create a Letterhead

PRACTICE GOAL TO ACCOMPLISH

Design the letterhead for a camera shop. Use a special typeface for the company name, a logo, and a line or box.

STRATEGIES TO CONSIDER

Before creating your letterhead, note the following suggestions for some basic design hints:

1. Developing a business image can be accomplished by using a special typeface. Try experimenting with several. (COACH'S TIP: You must have a purpose to use a special typeface and even then, remember to use it sparingly.)
2. Make the company name the focal point in your design. The name should be noticed first.

SUPPLIES TO USE

The following information should appear on your letterhead design.

NAME OF BUSINESS: *the Snap Shop*

ADDRESS: *7002 Flash Boulevard, Hillsboro, NH, 03244*

PHONE: *(555) 702-6930*

GRAPHIC IMAGE: *Use an old-fashioned camera.*

CHART TO FOLLOW

Use the following thumbnail sketch as a suggested layout for your letterhead design.

PLAYER'S NOTES:

Figure I.2 The practice drill page format lists the parts of each drill you need to complete.

Supplies to Use, and the *Chart to Follow*. The purpose of the format is to guide you in designing the document.

1. Read the *Practice Goal to Accomplish*, which identifies the type of document you are to design for the drill.
2. Read the list of *Strategies to Consider* relating to page layout and design that you should follow as you develop your publication.
3. Decide on your preplanning steps; analyze the target audience and finalize the publication requirements.
4. Complete your Planning Sheet form containing a thumbnail sketch and a list of the page setup requirements. See Figure I.3. These forms are found at the back of this text-workbook. Use the *Chart to Follow* as your guide for designing the document, or create your own design if the Coach approves. This form should be completed for each doc-

PLANNING SHEET

THUMBNAIL SKETCH:

Use this area to develop your idea for design.

Complete the following information pertaining to your layout.

STYLE SPECIFICATIONS:

PAGE SIZE: 8½ x 11" FILE NAME: Camera

MARGINS — TOP: ½" BOTTOM: ½" SIDES: ¾"

NUMBER OF COLUMNS: - SIZE: - GUTTER SIZE: -

TEXT (typeface, style, size):

the - Heidelberg 36pt.
Snap Shot - Heidelberg 48pt
Address - Geneva 14pt Bold
Phone - Geneva 12pt Bold

GRAPHICS (images, charts, illustrations):

Old fashion Camera

ENHANCEMENTS (lines, boxes, borders, screens):

1pt. line at top
6pt. line at bottom

Figure I.3 The Planning Sheet forms allow you to sketch a design and list the style specifications.

ument you design before you start working at the computer. The purpose of the form is to help you plan, organize, and maintain consistency in your document design.

5. Complete the Grid Sheet form by drawing your design to scale. See Figure I.4. These forms are also found at the back of this text-workbook. This form, too, should be completed for each document you design before you begin working at the computer. You will use this form to draw your design to scale. Its purpose is to provide you with a layout guide to follow as you work at the computer.
6. Use the *Player's Notes* section to jot down comments from the Coach or any points you want to remember relating to the drill.
7. Assemble the elements into the actual page layout (use information provided in the *Supplies to Use* section, or provide your own information if it is approved by the Coach).

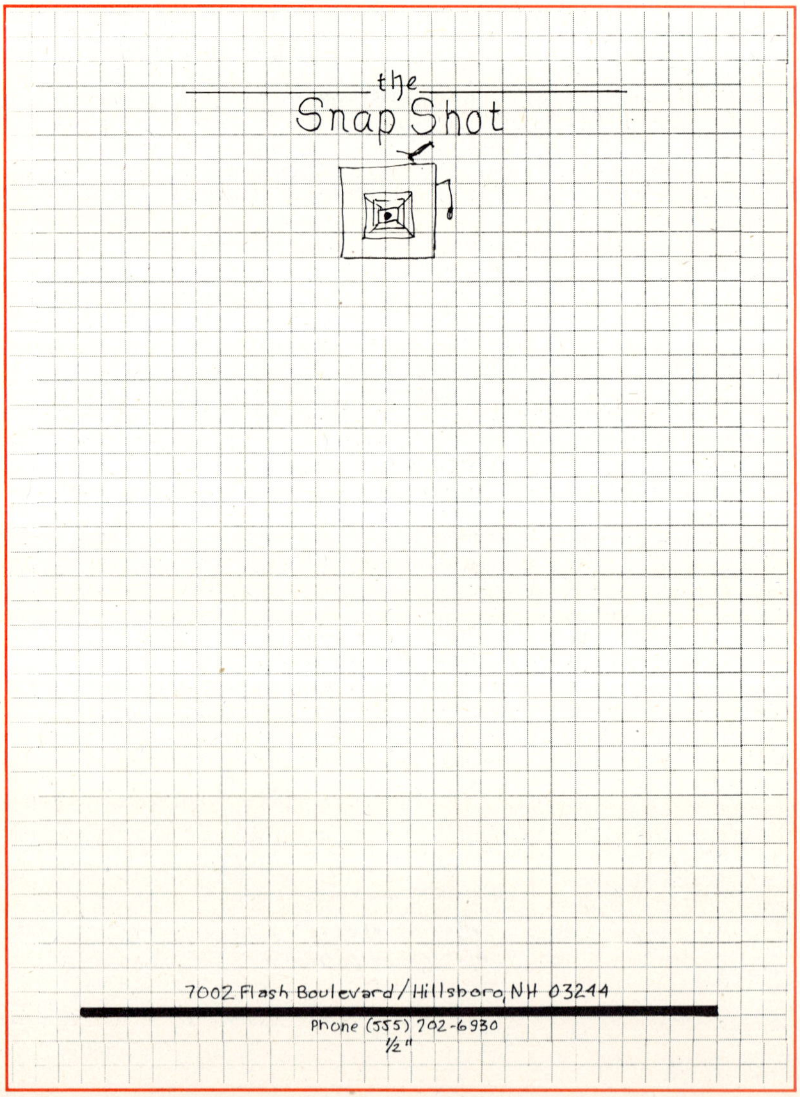

Figure I.4 The Grid Sheet forms allow you to more precisely plot the placement of elements of your document design.

8. Print a copy of the document. A sample completed printout of a document is shown in Figure I.5.
9. Save the file on your data disk.
10. Tear out the practice drill sheet in this book, place it with your planning sheet, grid sheet, and printout of the document; staple these papers together and hand them in to your Coach. (Or follow other directions given by the Coach for handing in your assignments.)

Drill D (Business Forms):

Follow the same steps as listed above for Drills A, B, and C with this one exception: In Drill D, the *Supplies to Use* section gives you an actual copy of a document currently being used in a business rather than just listing the information to be used. Your practice drill will be to "make over"

the Snap Shot

7002 Flash Boulevard / Hillsboro, NH 03244

Phone (555) 702-6930

Figure I.5 An example of a completed document shows how planning can affect your results.

(redesign) the existing document so that it communicates more effectively. You will attempt to add appeal to mundane business documents that were originated on a typewriter.

Part 4—The Games (Put DTP Skills into Action)

In *The Games*, which conclude the Publishing Season, you will participate in four games, each represented by a different company—Keystone Country Bank, The Tennis Club, Cruises and Tours International, and Spring Harbor County Fair. To play each game, you must design four documents for the company. This is your opportunity to demonstrate your mastery of DTP techniques because you will design these documents on your own. Remember to follow the DTP cycle as you complete each *play*.

For each of the plays, use the following steps:

1. Read the *Play to Execute*, which gives a description of the type of document to design as the play.
2. Complete your preplanning steps where you analyze the target audience and decide publication requirements.
3. Complete the Planning Sheet containing a thumbnail sketch and list the page setup requirements. There is no *Chart to Follow* section for the plays. You must make all the decisions in designing the document. Remember to apply the strategies you learned in *The Practice Drills*.
4. Complete the Grid Sheet by drawing your design to scale.
5. Use the *Player's Notes* section to jot down comments from the Coach or any points you want to remember relating to the play.
6. Assemble the elements into the actual page layout using the information from *Tactics to Include*. This section provides the information that should be contained in the document designed and developed during the play.
7. Print a copy of the document.
8. Save the file on your data disk.
9. Tear out the play sheet from this book, place it with your planning sheet, grid sheet, and printout of the document; staple these papers together and hand them in to your Coach. (Or follow other directions given by the Coach for handing in your assignments.) The outcome of the play is completely up to YOU! How will YOU design the document?

Each game contains the following plays:

1. Play A, which correlates to practice drill A (letterhead).
2. Play B, which correlates to practice drill B (flyers).
3. Play C, which correlates to practice drill C (speciality item).
4. Play D, which correlates to practice drill D (business forms).
5. An overtime section containing two additional plays that are optional.

HOW TO APPROACH THE DESKTOP PUBLISHING SEASON

Your Coach has been provided with several alternative schedules to use in directing the Publishing Season activities. However, unless instructed differently, you should progress through the Publishing Season as follows:

1. Read *The Ground Rules* to learn about the DTP field.
2. Complete all the tryout sessions in *The Game Fundamentals* to understand how to operate your DTP software.
3. Work through each of *The Practice Drills* to develop your DTP skills and learn design principles and layout techniques.
4. Complete one or more of *The Games* to demonstrate your talent for operating your DTP software to design publications effectively.

PART 1 The Ground Rules

OBJECTIVES

1. To become familiar with the ground rules of this simulation.
2. To understand the power of desktop publishing.
3. To look over desktop publishing equipment.
4. To learn more about getting started with your software.

INTRODUCTION

It's DTP season! Remember that DTP stands for DeskTop Publishing. And the *Coach* is anxious to sign up rookies for the team. This is your chance—you have always wanted to play on a team. Anyone interested in trying for the team must attend *The Ground Rules* meeting, which explains what the *DTP game* is, describes the *equipment* that's needed to play, and takes you on a tour of the *playing field* where the events will take place. The Coach is ready to begin, so let's head to the meeting!

UNDERSTANDING THE POWER OF DESKTOP PUBLISHING

At the meeting, the Coach is presenting the topic of desktop publishing. What do you think of when the term *desktop publishing* is mentioned? Do you think of *newsletter*? Or *computer*? Or *laser printer*? Or *graphics*? Any other terms? All these plus many others are involved in the field of desktop publishing.

Simply stated, **desktop publishing** (*DTP*) is the process of creating computer-generated publications that appear to have been professionally printed. Because DTP provides a means by which we communicate with one another, and because everyone is involved in communicating, we are all touched in some way by desktop publishing. See Figure 1.1. Desktop publishing begins with an idea you want to communicate to others. Think of communicating with desktop publishing as a game—*the DTP game.*

Figure 1.1 Desktop publishing provides a means by which we communicate with one another.
SOURCE: Courtesy of Apple Computer, Inc.

Planning a Publication

No matter what type of document is being created—manual, resume, memo, booklet, flyer—the information must be organized first. To be effective, a design should be developed before beginning at the computer.

Then, using DTP software—also called **page layout** or **page composition**—the text and graphics are assembled into the same page layout. **Text** refers to the words and numbers in a publication. **Graphics** are the illustrations and design elements. Text and graphics are the two primary elements of a publication.

Putting Together a Publication

With desktop publishing, you have flexibility. You can create the text and graphics right in the DTP software, or you can import the text files created with a word processing program along with the graphics from a clip art file or drawing and painting programs. A **clip art file** is a data file, usually stored on diskette, that contains graphic images that can be selected to put in a document. For example, if you want a picture of a sheep, you can find a piece of clip art and insert it in a publication. Figure 1.2 shows an example of some clip art.

Figure 1.2 Clip art is a graphic image that you can add to a publication.

A **drawing** or **painting program** is software that allows you to create the illustration to appear in your publication. With such a program you could draw your own sheep, for example, instead of using one from a clip art file.

Your publication can take shape in a variety of ways. Your creativity is your only limitation. Endless changes can be made in your design and the results seen in a matter of minutes.

Printing the Publication

As finishing touches are being added, you have the option of viewing the document on the screen in a **WYSIWYG format** (What-You-See-Is-What-You-Get). This means that the way things appear on the screen will be the way the page prints out. Once the design is finalized, a reproduction-quality copy of the publication is printed. In short, the desktop publishing cycle involves four steps:

1. Planning
2. Designing
3. Assembling
4. Printing

These steps comprise the DTP cycle for a publication created on a computer. The final printout begins with the idea to communicate to others. Along the way, designing and assembling the document must happen in order to reach the final step of printing.

LOOKING OVER DESKTOP PUBLISHING EQUIPMENT

To get started in desktop publishing, three basic kinds of equipment are needed to *play the game*: a personal computer, peripherals, and desktop publishing software. Equipment requirements are related to individual needs: What type of publications will be produced? Possibilities range from simple letterhead stationery or cards to sophisticated four-color brochures, magazines, or books. Once the requirements have been established, equipment is selected that corresponds to your needs.

Selecting a Personal Computer

For most desktop publishing systems, either an Apple or MS-DOS compatible personal computer is preferred. The Apple computer can be in either the Apple II or Macintosh format. The amount of memory determines the size and complexity of the documents that can be created; often 512K is a minimum. A hard disk drive is a recommended option, thus adding to the speed and ease of using the system. And if serious desktop publishing is desired, either a high-resolution or full-page monitor should be considered. Figures 1.3 and 1.4 show Apple and MS-DOS computers, respectively.

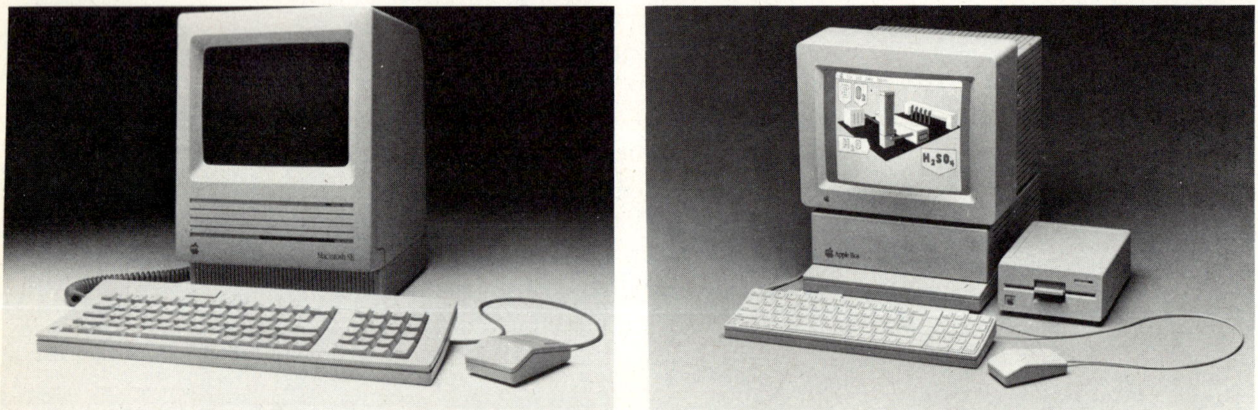

Figure 1.3 The Macintosh and the Apple IIgs can be used for desktop publishing.
SOURCE: Courtesy of Apple Computer, Inc.

Choosing Peripheral Devices

Peripheral devices are components that are external to the computer. For example, a printer and a modem are considered peripheral devices. As far as peripherals are concerned, a printer is required. Usually a laser printer is used because it can output high-quality documents that look like they were professionally typeset. If only rough-draft quality is needed, a dot-matrix printer is acceptable. Figure 1.5 shows different kinds of printers.

An optional peripheral device that can simplify the task of entering text or graphics into a layout is a **scanner**, which creates files that can be read by the computer. An example of a scanner is shown in Figure 1.6. A **mouse**, which controls cursor movement on the screen, is another desirable peripheral; some DTP software requires it. Usually the mouse will have one

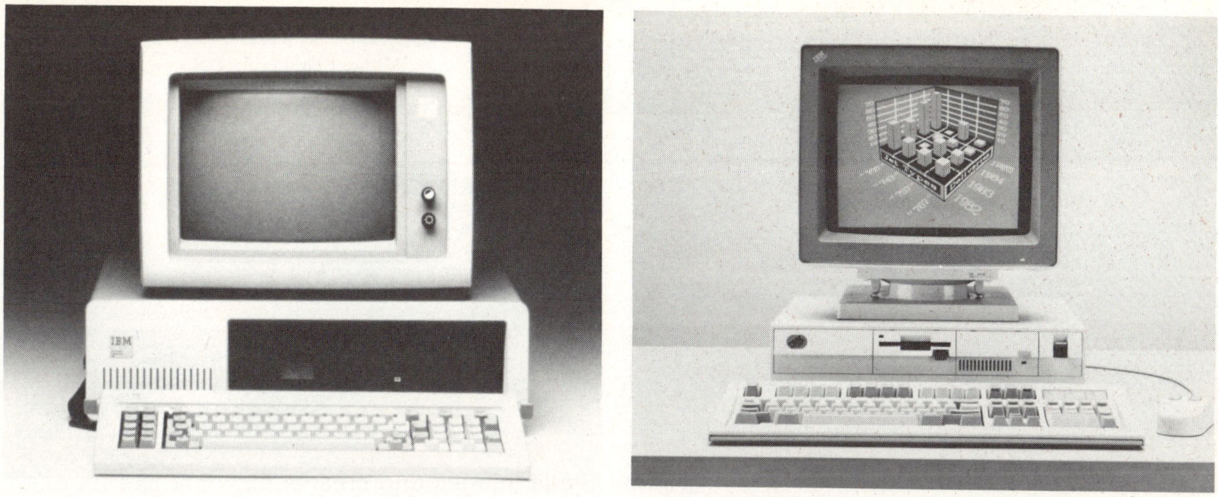

Figure 1.4 The IBM PC and the IBM Personal System/2 can be used for desktop publishing.
SOURCE: Courtesy of International Business Machines Corporation.

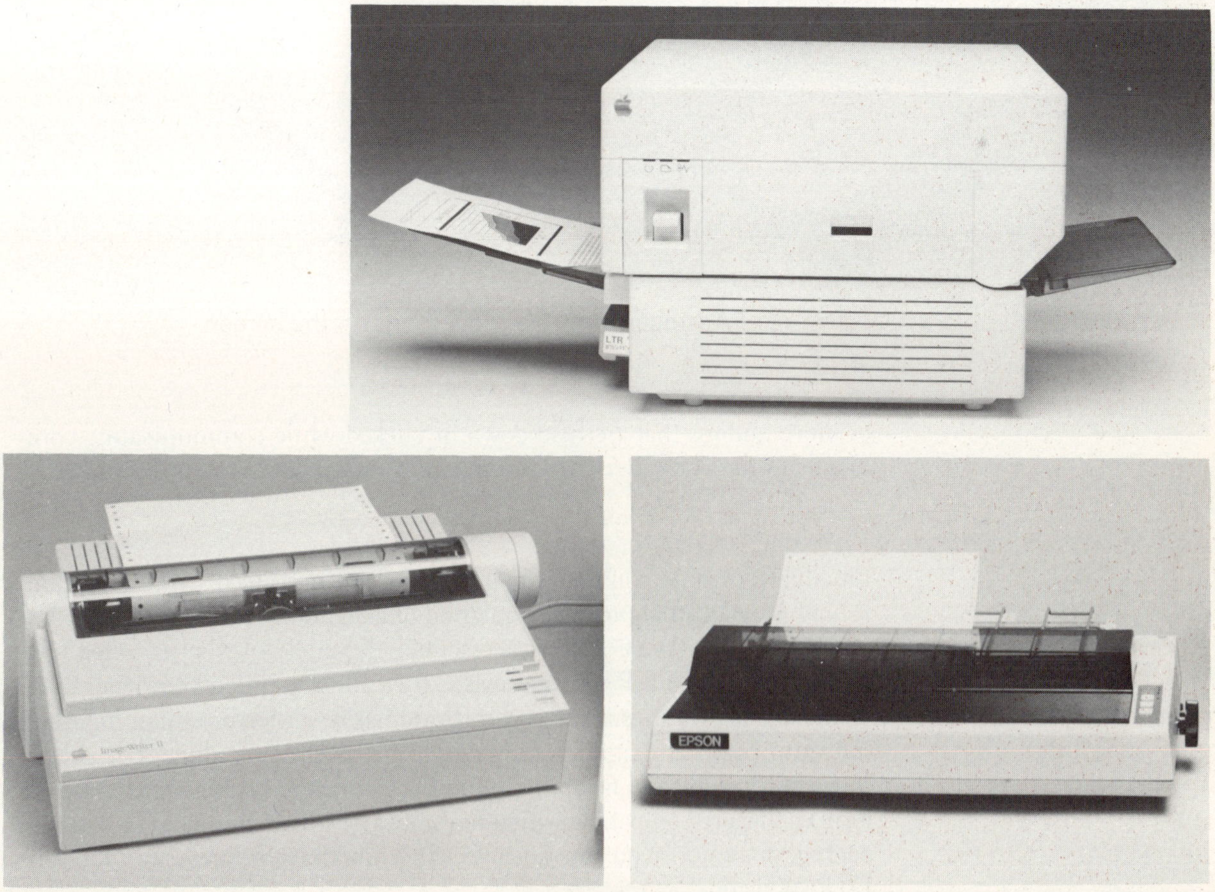

Figure 1.5 The desired quality of output determines whether a dot matrix or laser printer is used.
SOURCE: Top: Courtesy of Apple Computer, Inc.

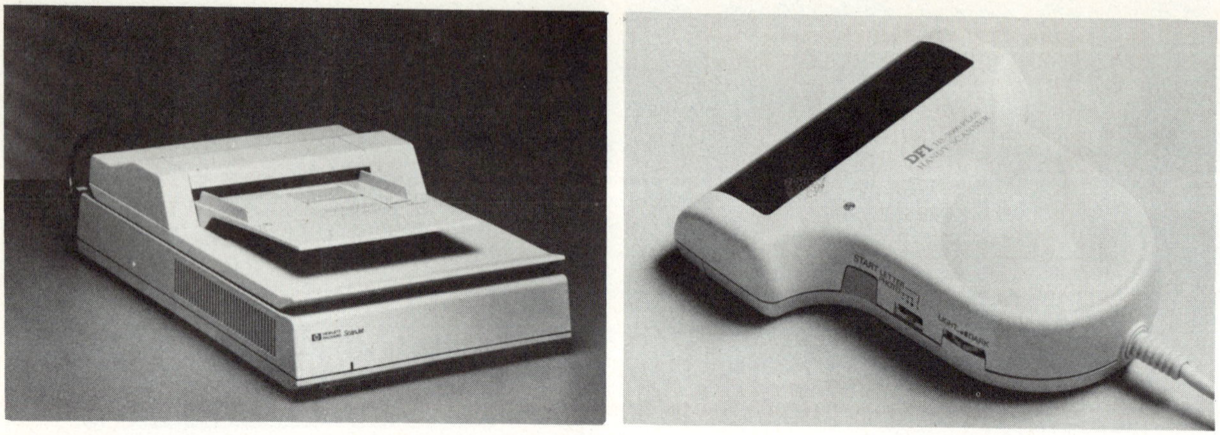

Figure 1.6 A scanner reads images and creates files that can be read by the computer.

SOURCE: Left: Courtesy Hewlett-Packard Company. Right: Photo courtesy of DFI Inc.

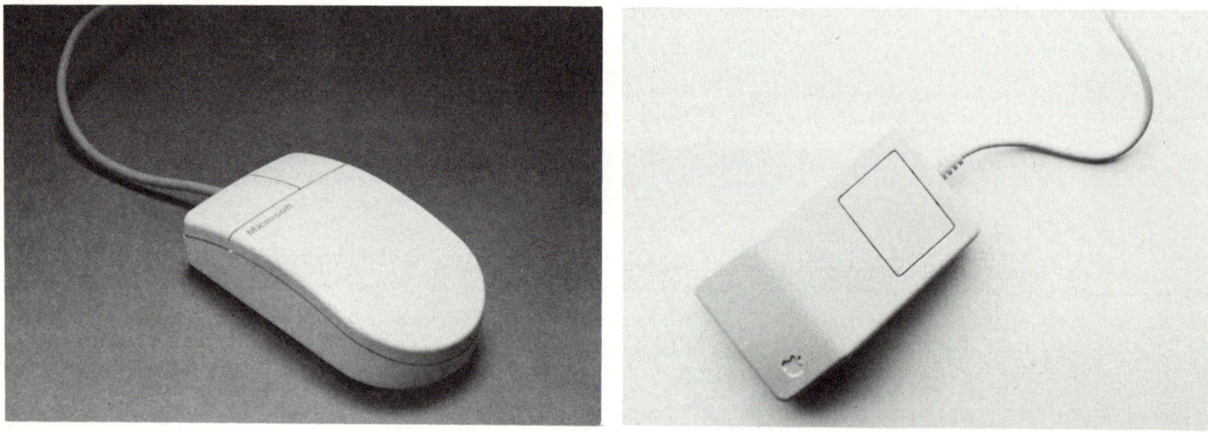

Figure 1.7 A mouse controls movement on the screen.

SOURCE: Right: © 1990 Apple Computer, Inc. Reprinted with Permission.

or more buttons that are held down or clicked while communicating commands to the computer. An example of a mouse is shown in Figure 1.7.

Determining the DTP Software to Use

Finally, you must consider what software you will need. A desktop publishing program that provides a method of assembling the page at the computer in a WYSIWYG format is essential. A variety of what is called low-end to high-end DTP software exists; basically the differences have to do with available features. **Low-end software** has fewer features than **high-end software**. Features that differ among software packages include style sheets, text wrap, speed, and flexibility. One DTP software package may offer file formats that are compatible with other software, while another DTP software package may not. You must decide what functions are necessary for your DTP software.

The cost of the DTP software should also be considered. Then check for compatibility with other types of software such as word processing, drawing, and painting programs. Because the software choice is based on matching the available features to individual requirements or needs, ask yourself these questions:

1. What DTP software features are needed?
2. What equipment is available?
3. What other kinds of software need to be supported—e.g., word processing software?
4. How much does the software cost?

Some popular DTP software packages include PageMaker, PFS:First Publisher, Springboard Publisher, Publish It!, Ready-Set-Go, and Ventura Publisher. There are many other DTP programs. This book is a **generic** book. This means that this text-workbook is designed to be used with many different kinds of DTP software. As you progress through these pages, you may run across tasks that are not possible with the software you have.

If this is the case, you may have to skip the particular exercise or find another way to perform the same task. Learning about the limitations of a software package is just as important as discovering the features.

GETTING STARTED WITH YOUR DESKTOP PUBLISHING SOFTWARE

First of all, it is a good idea for you to understand basic computer operating features such as (1) beginning and exiting a program, (2) using a mouse, (3) saving, deleting, and retrieving a file, and (4) functioning within a graphical user interface that uses such elements as windows, icons, menus, and scroll bars. See Figure 1.8. Once you are familiar with these types of tasks, you are ready to work with your desktop publishing software. Or, as the Coach likes to call it, the *playing field*.

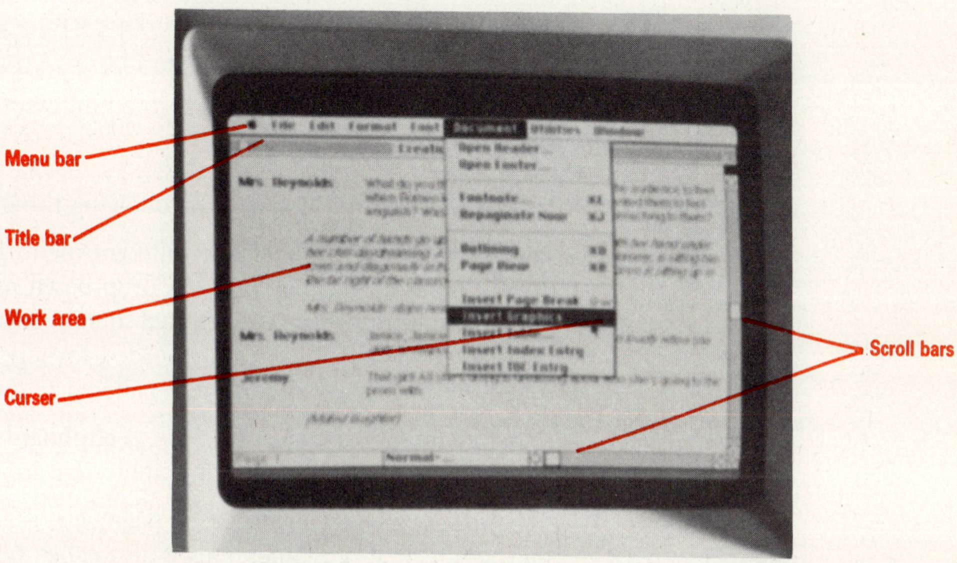

Figure 1.8 A window environment is a typical feature of graphical user interfaces.

SOURCE: © 1990 Apple Computer, Inc. Reprinted with permission.

Getting started with an individual software package involves finding the answers to several types of questions and then experimenting with what you see on the screen. During this process, it may be necessary for you to refer to your software reference manual. Typical questions relating to the software might be the following:

1. Is on-line help available? **On-line help** is a feature of the software that provides detailed information about performing specific tasks while working within the software.
2. Can files be imported from other software packages? Which packages?
3. Are style sheets or master pages available? **Style sheets** or **master pages** are features of the software that provide suggested page layout designs or page formats.
4. Are operations performed using the keyboard, a mouse, or both?

Once these types of questions are answered, you will load the program and explore the main screen to familiarize yourself with what you see there. Look for these typical features:

1. **Work area**—the place on the screen where your layout of the document is done.
2. **Scroll bars**—bars along two sides of the screen that enable you to move the page horizontally or vertically to access a different part of the document.
3. **Rulers**—a horizontal ruler across the top of the screen and a vertical ruler down the left side of screen used to position objects on the page.
4. **Menu bar**—a list of the program options available.
5. **Title bar**—displays name of the file that is currently open.
6. **Tool box**—contains **icons** (small symbolic pictures) representing the tools that can be selected when working with text or graphics.
7. **Cursor**—the blinking pointer on the screen indicating where the action will take place. The cursor can take on different shapes depending on the task being performed.

Also, it is important to know the following things:

1. How to maneuver through the different menu features such as drop-down menus and dialog boxes. A **drop-down menu** provides a list of available choices within the selected menu bar item, and a **dialog box** asks for additional information needed to perform the desired command. A drop-down menu is also called a *pull-down menu*.
2. Whether there is a clipboard feature. A **clipboard** is a temporary holding area for the most recent text or graphics cut from the document.
3. What page views are available. A **page view** is a page that is displayed on the screen at one time. This is also called *page mode* or *looking at the whole page*. What page view sizes are available?
4. How to move to another page.

5. Whether frames are used in designing a document. A **frame** is an area or container created to hold and position text and/or graphic elements on the page. This varies with DTP packages.

COACH'S CORNER

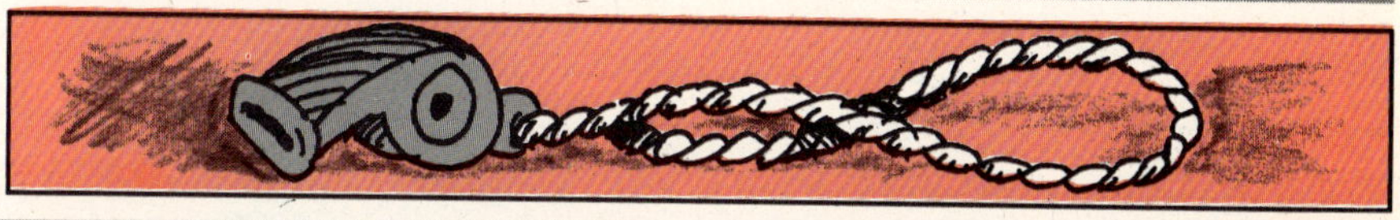

One reminder from the Coach: At this point, this is just a general overview of what you might explore as you experiment a little with your software. So far, your goal is merely to be aware of what is available with your individual DTP program. Once you feel comfortable, move on to Part 2, *The Game Fundamentals* sections, where you will actually begin working with specific features of DTP software.

CLASS HOUR: ______ DATE: ______ NAME: ______________________

THE *Ground Rules* QUIZ

Directions: Complete the following statements and answer the questions.

1. The two primary elements of a publication are ______________________
   and ______________________.
2. *WYSIWYG* is the acronym for ______________________.
3. The required peripheral for desktop publishing is a ______________________.
4. Are most DTP systems either MS-DOS or Apple? Yes or no. ______________________
5. What are the 3 basic kinds of equipment needed for desktop publishing?
   a. ______________________
   b. ______________________
   c. ______________________
6. A ____________ printer produces documents that look like they were professionally typeset.
7. Must the text and graphics used in a publication be created in your DTP software only? Yes or no.
   ____
8. Two optional types of DTP peripherals are a ______________________
   and a ______________________.
9. Define desktop publishing.
   ____
   ____
   ____
10. Identify two basic differences between low-end and high-end DTP software.
    a. ______________________
    b. ______________________
11. Another name for desktop publishing software is ______________________.

12. The 4 steps in the DTP cycle are:

a. ______________________________

b. ______________________________

c. ______________________________

d. ______________________________

13. Is everyone touched in some way by desktop publishing? Yes or no. ______________

14. Identify three typical features that might be displayed on the screen when using DTP software.

a. ______________________________

b. ______________________________

c. ______________________________

15. A temporary holding area for the most recent text or graphics cut from the document is called a ______________________________.

PART 2 The Game Fundamentals

OBJECTIVES

1. To determine the page setup.
2. To work with graphic files.
3. To use graphic drawing tools.
4. To work with text.
5. To assemble a page.
6. To print a document.

INTRODUCTION

Tryout time is here! This means that your goal is to learn how to operate your desktop publishing software effectively so you can earn a position on the DTP team. This part is called *The Game Fundamentals* because in this section you become familiar with as much about the basics of your DTP software as you can.

In the *Tryout Sessions*, you will complete activities that provide practice using the basic features and options of a desktop publisher. The following topics are included in your practice: learning DTP terminology, determining the page setup, working with graphic files, using graphic drawing tools, working with text, assembling a page, printing the publication, and preplanning your document.

Remember, as you progress through this training period, the Coach is evaluating your performance and selecting players for the DTP team. Player selection is based on the successful completion of the different activities. As you work through each task, feel free to repeat any step you have difficulty with until you understand how to execute the technique. For future reference, keep a record of the keystrokes and/or commands you use to complete each task.

There's the whistle. The first tryout session is ready to begin!

CLASS HOUR: ______ DATE: ______ NAME: ____________________

TRYOUT SESSION 1

Determining the Page Setup

Page setup refers to the development of a page format, often called the *blueprint*. This is the underlying framework used when constructing a publication. A basic blueprint establishes the page size, margins, number of columns and the type specifications (in inches, decimals, or picas, depending on your DTP software).

TERMINOLOGY

Learning to develop effective publications at the computer will involve learning new terms. You will begin by becoming familiar with some of the following terms relating to the page setup.

Alignment — How text appears in the column (flush left, flush right, centered, or justified).

Ascender — The part of a character of type that extends above the letter. For example, the lowercase letter *h*.

Default — A value or setting automatically used by your software program unless instructed differently by the operator.

Descender — The part of a character of type that descends below the letter. For example, the lowercase letter *g*.

Font — A complete set of letters, numbers, and symbols in a single typeface and size.

Gutter — The space between columns of text or inside margin for binding.

Landscape — A page layout orientation that is wider than it is tall.

Layout — The arrangement of elements (graphics and text) on a page.

Leading — The space between lines of type.

Margins — The white space at the top, sides, and bottom of a publication.

Pica — A unit of measurement commonly used in the printing industry. Six picas equals approximately one inch.

Point — The smallest unit of measurement; 72 points equals one inch. Type is measured in points.

Portrait — A page layout orientation that is taller than it is wide.

Ruler Guides — Nonprinting horizontal and vertical measuring lines that can be used to position and/or align elements on the page layout.

Sans Serif — A typeface without fine cross-lines at the top and bottom of the main stroke of the characters.

Serif — A typeface with a fine cross-line at the top and bottom of the main stroke of the characters.

Spread — A left- and right-hand page viewed together (two facing pages).

Typeface — A set of characters (letters, numbers, and symbols) that share the same design. (This is sometimes erroneously called a *font*.)

Type Size — The measurement of the typeface; the distance between the top of the ascender and the bottom of the descender.

Type Style — A variation in the enhancement of the typeface (e.g., **boldface** or *italics*).

TRYOUT SESSION GOALS

Now read the following goals and complete the tryout session where you practice selecting the different page setup options available in your DTP software.

1. Selecting the desired page size for the publication.
2. Setting the required margins.
3. Defining the number of columns in the layout.
4. Choosing type specifications for the text.

TRYOUT SESSION

To begin this tryout session, open a new document with your software package. Determine the page setup defaults for your DTP software and write them below for your reference. You may need to ask your instructor for help.

Page Size: ________________

Margins:

- Top Margin ________________
- Bottom Margin ________________
- Left Margin ________________
- Right Margin ________________

Number of Columns: ________________

Gutter Width: ________________

Type Specification:

- Typeface ________________
- Type Size ________________
- Type Style ________________

Complete each of the following steps. The page size and margins are indicated in inches, so it may be necessary for you to convert the inches to a different measurement standard (letter, legal, picas, decimals, etc.) for your software. On the blank lines, write the keystrokes and/or commands used to perform the page setup options. The answers will vary depending on your DTP software package. Some items listed may be your software's default values. Indicate if the option is not available to you.

1. Select a portrait page size of 8½ by 11 inches for your layout orientation. (Goal 1)

____

2. Try selecting a different portrait page size for your layout orientation; for example, 5½ by 8½ inches, 8½ by 14 inches, or other. (Goal 1)

____

3. Now try a landscape page size of 11 by 8½ inches for your layout orientation. (Goal 1)

____

4. Return to a page size of 8½ by 11 inches. (Goal 1)

____

5. Set the following margins. (Goal 2)

a. Top margin = 1 inch ______________________________

b. Bottom margin = ½ inch ______________________________

c. Both right and left margins = ¾ inch ______________________________

6. Try changing your margins to the following. (Goal 2)

a. Top margin = 1¼ inch ______________________________

b. Bottom margin = ¾ inch ______________________________

c. Left side margin = 1½ inch ______________________________

d. Right side margin = ⅝ inch ______________________________

7. Adjust margins once again as follows. (Goal 2)

a. Top margin = 1½ inch ______________________________

b. Bottom margin = 1 inch ______________________________

c. Both right and left margins = 1 inch ______________________________

8. Now establish the following setup for the columns. (Goal 3)

a. Number of columns = 2 ______

b. Width of each column = 3 inches ______

c. Gutter between columns = ½ inch ______

9. Let's try a different column setup. (Goal 3)

a. Number of columns = 5 ______

b. Width of each column = 1 inch ______

c. Gutter between columns = ⅜ inch ______

10. One last time, adjust the columns to the following. (Goal 3)

a. Number of columns = 3 ______

b. Width of each column = 2 inches ______

c. Gutter between columns = ¼ inch ______

11. Select a serif typeface with the following. (Goal 4)

a. Point size = 10 ______

b. Leading = 13 ______

c. Type style = normal ______

d. Text alignment = justified ______

12. And finally, select a sans serif typeface with the following. Your point sizes may vary depending on the typeface you use. (Goal 4)

a. Point size = 18 ______

b. Leading = 23 ______

c. Type style = bold ______

d. Text alignment = centered ______

You do not need to save this tryout document, but you may want to use it for future reference. If so, please save it on your own formatted data disk.

CLASS HOUR: ______ DATE: ______ NAME: ______________________

TRYOUT SESSION 2

Working with Graphic Files

Graphics is everything printed on your page except the words (text), and even words can be considered graphics at times. You will begin by working with graphic files (clip art or graphic images). Graphics can add interest and life to a publication; but remember that your graphic message must have a focal point and that too many graphics tend to clutter a design.

TERMINOLOGY

Working with graphic files is easy and fun. Before you start, however, review the following terms so you will understand what each step is directing you to do.

Clip Art — Ready-made graphic images (pictures, illustrations, symbols, etc.) saved to a file that can be retrieved and placed in a document. These files come in a variety of formats, depending on the software involved.

Clipboard — A temporary holding area for the graphics or text that was last cut or copied in the layout.

Copy — To duplicate a graphic image or text to place in another location.

Crop — To eliminate an unwanted area of a graphic image.

Cut — To remove a graphic image or text from the present position on the page, thus allowing it to be moved elsewhere or deleted.

Flip — To turn the graphic image in the opposite direction horizontally or vertically.

Paste — To anchor the graphic image or text in a new location; sometimes called stamping with graphic images.

Resize — To increase or decrease the size of a graphic image.

Reverse — To switch to the opposite background display; e.g., if the background is black, to change it to white and vice versa. Sometimes this is called *inverting*.

Rotate — To turn the graphic image 90 degrees.

TRYOUT SESSION GOALS

Now read the following goals and complete the tryout session where you practice working with graphic files using your DTP software.

1. Selecting the graphic image to use.
2. Positioning a graphic image on the page.
3. Modifying the present graphic image.
4. Copying a graphic image to another location.
5. Moving a graphic image to a new location.
6. Erasing graphic images from the page.

TRYOUT SESSION

To begin this tryout session, open a new document using your default page setup or the following page setup:

A page size of 8½ by 11 inches
1 inch top, bottom, and side margins
1 column layout

Complete each of the following steps. Write the keystrokes and/or commands you use to perform each graphic file technique. The answers will vary depending on your DTP software. Indicate if the technique is not available to you.

1. Select any clip art (or the one designated by your coach) to work with and bring it into your layout. Depending on your software, you may have to load the art as a special file. (Goal 1)

___

2. Position the clip art approximately in the center of your screen. (Goal 2)

___

3. Make the following changes to the clip art that is in your layout. When you want to work with a graphic image that is already in your page layout, remember that you must select the graphic image you wish to work with—usually by placing the cursor on it or placing a selection box or rule around it. (Goal 3)

a. First, resize the clip art, enlarging it to twice its current size.

___

b. Now reduce it back to its original size.

___

c. Let's try to enlarge the clip art horizontally, then return it to its original shape.

___

d. This time you will enlarge the clip art vertically only.

e. What about flipping the clip art? Try flipping it horizontally and then flip it back.

f. Can you vertically flip the clip art? Now flip it back.

g. Is it possible to reverse or invert the clip art? If so, reverse it and then change it back.

h. Let's try rotating the clip art. Rotate it back to its original position.

i. Finally, crop the clip art so you have only the top half of the original clip art on the screen.

4. Isn't it neat how you can make all those changes to your original clip art! And besides being easy to do, it happens almost instantly. Now you will make copies of the clip art as follows. (Goal 4)

a. Copy the clip art and place the new copy below the original clip art.

b. Let's make another copy of the clip art; this time place the new copy on the left side of the original clip art.

5. Finally, pick up the desired clip art and move it to a different location on the page. (Goal 5)

a. Select the original clip art, move it to the top right corner of the screen.

b. Now select one of the other clip art copies and move it near the bottom of the page.

6. You do not need to save this tryout document, but you may want to use it for future reference. If so, please save it to your own formatted data disk. Otherwise, erase all copies of the clip art. (Goal 6)

7. Optional: Import graphic files from other software packages. Experiment with this feature if it is available to you.

COACH'S CORNER

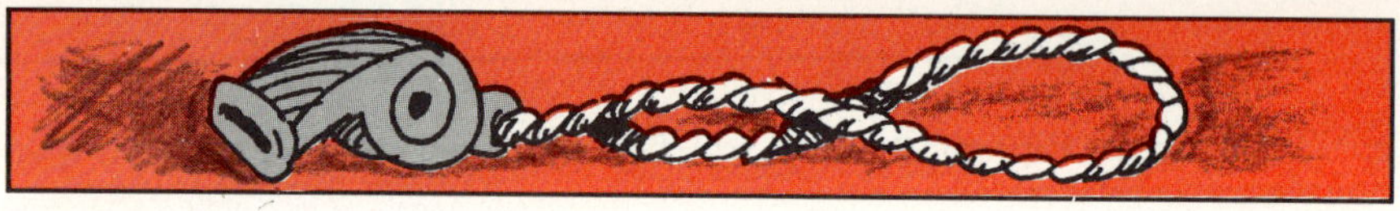

Isn't working with graphics fun? As you can see, lots of interesting things are possible with graphic images; just stretch your imagination and see what you can come up with. To continue your conditioning in the area of graphics, you will practice with several graphic tools in your next tryout session. These tools are used to add enhancements to the documents.

PLAYER'S NOTES:

CLASS HOUR: ______ DATE: ________ NAME: ______________________________

TRYOUT SESSION 3

Using Graphic Drawing Tools

Graphic tools are used to add enhancements to your page layout. Your second graphic practice will include working with several drawing tools: lines, boxes, circles, and freehand—which are used to create the different enhancements.

TERMINOLOGY

Let's look at some of the terms pertaining directly to the graphic drawing tools.

Border — A line or frame surrounding graphics, graphs, illustrations, photographs, text, etc., that defines the edges. Borders can be simple or elaborate.

Box Rule — A line that has four sides to form a box. A box rule usually surrounds text or graphics.

Fill Pattern — Various patterns from clear to opaque used to change the background of a defined shape; also called a *paint bucket* or *shades*.

Hairline — The thinnest possible line your software can produce. A hairline is often used to define columns. It can be used as a vertical or horizontal rule.

Rule — A line of varying thickness from hairline to wide. You may be able to select the thickness of the rule with your software.

Screen — A pattern of dots from solid black to various levels of gray. Screens are described in percentages; 100% is solid black. A screen adds a tint to a defined area for special emphasis. This concept is similar to a fill pattern, only you do not have elaborate patterns—only patterns of dots. Screens are also referred to as *shades*.

TRYOUT SESSION GOALS

Now read the following goals and complete the tryout session where you experiment with different drawing tools available in your DTP software.

1. Placing the cursor where drawing will begin.
2. Selecting the drawing tool and width.
3. Creating your own drawing.
4. Making modifications to the drawing.

5. Moving the drawing to a different page location.
6. Making a copy of your drawing.
7. Erasing the drawing.

TRYOUT SESSION

To begin this tryout session, open a new document using your default page setup or the following page setup:

A page size of 8½ by 11 inches
1-inch top, bottom, and side margins
1-column layout

Complete each of the following steps. Write the keystrokes and/or commands you use working with each drawing tool. The answer will vary depending on your DTP software. Indicate if the option is not available to you.

Graphic Drawing Tool: Line

1. Position the cursor at the center point of the screen. (Goal 1)

___

2. Select the line drawing tool and indicate its width, if necessary. (Goal 2)

___

3. Now try drawing a 2-inch horizontal line by moving the cursor to the point where you want your line to end. (Goal 3)

___

4. Draw a vertical line this time. Make it approximately 3 inches long and on the left side of your screen. (Goals 1, 2 & 3)

___

5. Let's change the length of the 2-inch horizontal line and try to make it a 3-inch line instead. (Goal 4)

___

6. What about the width of the vertical line? How can you make the present line thicker? (Goal 4)

___

7. Now pick up the horizontal line and move it to the top of the screen. (Goal 5)

___

8. Finally copy the vertical line and place this copy on the right side of the screen. (Goal 6)

___

9. Erase the lines. (Goal 7)

___

Graphic Drawing Tool: Box Rule

1. Position the cursor at the center point of the screen. This will be the upper left corner of your box. (Goal 1)

2. Select the box drawing tool and indicate its width, if necessary. (Goal 2)

3. Draw a 3-inch box by moving the cursor diagonally to the lower right corner of the box. (Goal 3)

4. Try changing the size of your box; let's decrease it to a 2-inch box instead of the 3-inch size. (Goal 4)

5. Now pick up the box and move it to the top right corner of the screen. (Goal 5)

6. Make a copy of the box and place this copy in the top left corner of the screen. (Goal 6)

7. Let's draw another box, but this time make it rectangular. Position it in the middle of the screen. (Goals 1, 2 & 3)

8. If possible, modify the rectangular box so it contains a fill pattern or screen. (Goal 4)

9. Bring a graphic image into the layout, position it in the bottom right corner of the screen, and draw a box around the graphic image. (Goals 1, 2 & 3)

10. Erase the graphic image and all boxes. (Goal 7)

Graphic Drawing Tool: Circles

1. Position the cursor at the center point of the screen. (Goal 1)

2. Select the circle drawing tool and indicate its width, if necessary. Some software has a special tool for drawing circles. For example, some software has a shape command. If your software does not have this feature, try loading a circular border as clip art and then modify it. (Goal 2)

3. Try drawing a 2-inch circle. A circle should form as you move the cursor to the other side of the circle. (Goal 3)

4. Let's change the size of the circle; enlarge it to a 3-inch circle instead of 2 inches. (Goal 4)

___

5. Now pick up the circle and move it to the lower left corner of the screen. (Goal 5)

___

6. Finally, place a copy of the circle in the upper right corner of the screen. (Goal 6)

___

7. Erase the circles. (Goal 7)

___

Graphic Drawing Tool: Freehand

1. Position the cursor where you want the drawing to begin. (Goal 1)

___

2. Select the freehand drawing tool and indicate its width, if necessary. (Goal 2)

___

3. As you move the cursor around on the screen, you will be creating your own design. (Goal 3)

___

4. Now change the width of the drawing tool and continue your drawing. (Goal 4)

___

5. Let's try moving part of your drawing to a different location on the screen. (Goal 5)

___

6. Try flipping part of your drawing either horizontally or vertically. (Goal 4)

___

7. Make a copy of part of your drawing and place it somewhere else on the screen. (Goal 6)

___

8. Erase the drawing (Goal 7).

___

Miscellaneous Drawing Tools

Experiment with other drawing tools available with your software: text as graphics, boxes with rounded corners, ovals, etc.

You do not need to save this tryout document, but you may want to use it for future reference. If so, please save it to your own formatted data disk.

CLASS HOUR: ______ DATE: ______ NAME: ______________________

TRYOUT SESSION 4

Working with Text

As mentioned before, text refers to the printed words on the page which can include body copy, headlines, subheads, captions, headers, footers, and page numbers. Your practice will basically include working with body copy. However, realize that the other kinds of text also use these same techniques. Text contains the message of the publication and occupies a majority of the page. So, be sure it is easy to read.

TERMINOLOGY

You will have a better understanding of what to expect when working with text if you review the following terms. Some of the words may be familiar to you if you have used a word processor.

Body Copy — The main text in a document. Body copy does not include headings.

Bold — Type that is heavier and darker in appearance than regular or normal type; also called *boldface*.

Caption — Text used to describe an illustration or photograph. Sometimes captions are numbered.

Centering — Aligning text evenly between the left and right margins.

DTP Text Editor — The word processor in your desktop publishing software that allows you to work with text. This is also called a *word processor* or *editing text*.

Edit — To make corrections and/or changes (add to or delete from) the existing text.

Flush Left — Aligning text with the left margin (also called *left-justified*).

Flush Right — Aligning text with the right margin (also called *right-justified*).

Footer — Text and a page number at the bottom of each page.

Header — Text and a page number at the top of each page.

Headline — Text in large type that calls attention to the body copy.

Highlighting — To cause the text block to appear in reverse video. Highlighting defines the area to be formatted or changed; also called *selecting* or *choosing an area or block*.

Italics — A typeface variation that is slanted to the right.

Justified — Aligning text with both the left and right margin even.

Page View — The portion of a page that is displayed on the screen at one time. You can also see the entire page on the screen. This is also called *zooming, showing a page, viewing a page,* or a *text mode window.*

Subheads — Headings that follow headlines for covering more detailed topics in the body copy.

Text Block — An identified section of text such as a word, a line, a sentence, a paragraph, or a column. This section of text has been highlighted.

Text Flow — Text automatically continuing from the bottom of one column to the top of the next column.

Text Wrap — Adjusting the appearance of text to follow the shape of an encountered graphic. The text formats around an illustration. This is also called *picturewrap* or *wrapping text.*

TRYOUT SESSION GOALS

Now read the following goals and complete the tryout session where you practice working with the text features available with your DTP software.

1. Creating a text block using the DTP text editor.
2. Editing the text block for corrections or changes.
3. Copying a text block to a different location.
4. Removing a text block from the layout.
5. Modifying the appearance of a text block.
6. Combining a graphic image with a text block.

TRYOUT SESSION

To begin this tryout session, open a new document and establish the following page setup:

A page size of 8½ by 11 inches
1-inch top, bottom, and side margins
3-column layout (columns 2 inches wide with a ¼ inch gutter)
12-point serif typeface

Complete each of the following steps. Write the keystrokes and/or commands you use to perform each text-related feature. The answers will vary depending on your DTP software. Indicate if the feature is not available to you.

1. Using your DTP text editor to key directly into your page layout, create a text block that contains the paragraph at the beginning of this tryout session. It's headed WORKING WITH TEXT. Just key that first paragraph to use as your sample paragraph. The first line starts with *As mentioned before...* Do not go any further than the terminology section. (Goal 1)

a. Move the cursor around within the block of text. Understand how to manipulate your location on the screen. Notice that you CANNOT move the cursor beyond where text has been entered.

____

b. Edit your copy, correct any keying errors you find as you proofread through the text.

____

2. Add more text to the present paragraph. (Goal 2)

a. Insert the following words in the first sentence: Before the words "body copy," add *the following:* (use two spaces). Before the word "header," add *jumplines, pull quotes,*

____

b. Now insert the following sentence before the last sentence in the paragraph: *Entering text into your layout can be accomplished by using your DTP text editor or importing previously created text files.*

____

c. Finally, insert a 5-space paragraph indention at the beginning of the paragraph.

____

3. Editing also can involve deleting text from the existing paragraph. You may need to highlight the words to delete in a paragraph. (Goal 2)

a. Delete the words you entered in Step 2a. ______________________________

b. Now delete the sentence you entered in Step 2b. ______________________________

4. Let's try copying your paragraph. When you want to work with a block of text that is already in your page layout, remember that you must identify (select) the text block you wish to work with—usually by highlighting the desired text. (Goal 3)

a. Place the copy of the paragraph at the end of the current text block.

____

b. Continue copying the paragraph and place it at the end until your text fills the first, second, and part of the third columns.

____

c. Did text flow to the next column automatically (yes/no)? ______________________________

d. If you answered no, what must you do for text to continue in the next column?

____

5. Practice moving the cursor around within your three columns of text. (Selecting a page view of the full page may be helpful while doing the following.)

a. Jump between the columns. ______________________________

b. Try to jump to the end of a column. ______________________________

c. Jump to the beginning of a different column. ____________________

d. Now go to the end of the page. ____________________

e. Return to the beginning of the page. ____________________

6. Let's remove all the text in column 3. Delete it in one step as a text block. (Goal 4)

____

7. Make the following modifications in the appearance of the text. (Goal 5)

a. Change the alignment of the text in the first column to the following:

Make the text appear flush right. ____________________

Now justify the text. ____________________

Try to center the text. ____________________

Finally make the text flush left. ____________________

b. Change the type style of the text in the first sentence to the following:

Make the text a bold type style. ____________________

Now change the text to italics. ____________________

c. Change the type specifications of the text in both columns to the following:

A sans serif typeface ____________________

A 10-point type size ____________________

d. Change your three-column layout to a two-column layout. What happens to the text?

____

e. Once again, copy the first paragraph and continue placing it at the end of the text block until the first column and half of the second are filled with text.

____

8. Try placing a graphic image in the layout along with your text. (Goal 6)

a. Position a small graphic image in the middle of the first column of text. What happens to the text?

____

b. Text can be aligned in different ways in relation to the graphic image. Adjust the alignment of text in the following ways

Make the text wrap around the graphic image. ____________________

Now place the text above and below the graphic image. ____________________

Have the text appear on only one side of the graphic image. ____________________

Finally, let the text flow over the top of the graphic image. ____________________

c. Let's move the graphic image to a location between column 1 and column 2. Now adjust the alignment of the text so it wraps around the graphic image from both columns.

____

d. Move the graphic image so it is in column 2 only. Then enlarge the graphic image to the exact width of the column with the text appearing above and below the graphic image.

____

e. Now try drawing a hairline rule in the gutter between column 1 and column 2.

____

9. You do not need to save this tryout document, but you may want to use it for future reference. If so, please save it to your own formatted data disk. Otherwise, clear the screen.

10. Optional: Try importing text files from a different word processing software package into your DTP software package. Experiment with this feature, if it is available to you.

____

____

COACH'S CORNER

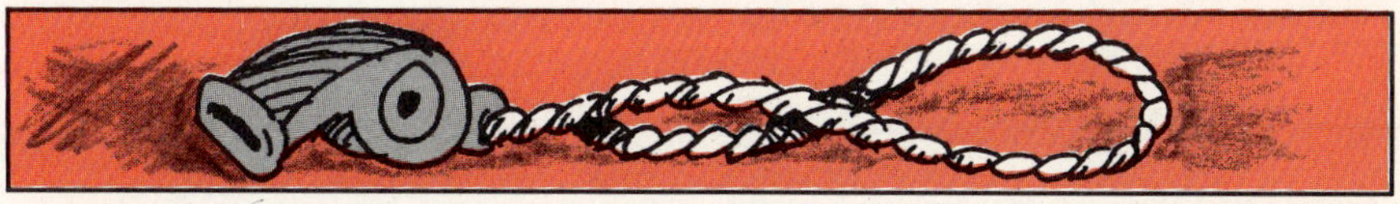

That was a long practice for one session, so let's take a time out! During this break, try running through the graphics and text drills again to be sure you can easily execute all the commands yourself.

Now—ready to continue? As you tackle the next tryout session, you will be challenging the real muscle of desktop publishing—combining text and graphics into the same file.

PLAYER'S NOTES:

CLASS HOUR: ______ DATE: ______ NAME: ______________________

TRYOUT SESSION 5

Assembling a Page

Page assembly refers to placing previously created text and graphic elements into a predefined page setup. Once the elements are on the page, it may be necessary to make modifications and/or add enhancements to complete the design. Remember, your goal is to design a publication that will convince the *looker* to be a *reader* of your message.

TERMINOLOGY

Once you know how to work with text and graphics, you are ready to start assembling publications—the true purpose and/or function of desktop publishing. The terms involved in this process are defined below; refer to the list as needed.

Element — A unit (either an illustration/graphic or type/text) to be used in a publication.

Graphic — An illustration created using a graphic software file or a shape drawn with graphic tools.

Live Area — The space on the page layout between the margins where text and graphic elements are placed.

Masthead — A consistent design that creates an identity for the title, logo, and related information that appears on each issue of a newsletter.

Pull Quote — A short phrase or sentence pulled from an article and set in a larger size type than the body text.

Rough — A preliminary sketch to scale of where the elements will appear in a layout.

Style Sheet — A file containing the type specifications and format information for a page design; can be used with different documents.

Text — Words, numbers, and symbols that present information.

Thumbnail Sketch — A rough version of the page design rendered in miniature.

White Space — The area on a page where no text or graphic is placed.

WYSIWYG — The acronym for *What-You-See-Is-What-You-Get*.

TRYOUT SESSION GOALS

Now read the following goals and complete the tryout session where you will actually assemble your first publication.

1. Establishing the page setup requirements.
2. Placing the text and graphic elements in the layout.
3. Editing, modifying, and adjusting the elements as needed.
4. Adding enhancements to the layout design.
5. Accepting a final design for the publication.
6. Saving the file to the disk.

TRYOUT SESSION

To begin this tryout session, refer to the rough sketch (Figure 2.1) of the page design you will be assembling as you complete each of the following

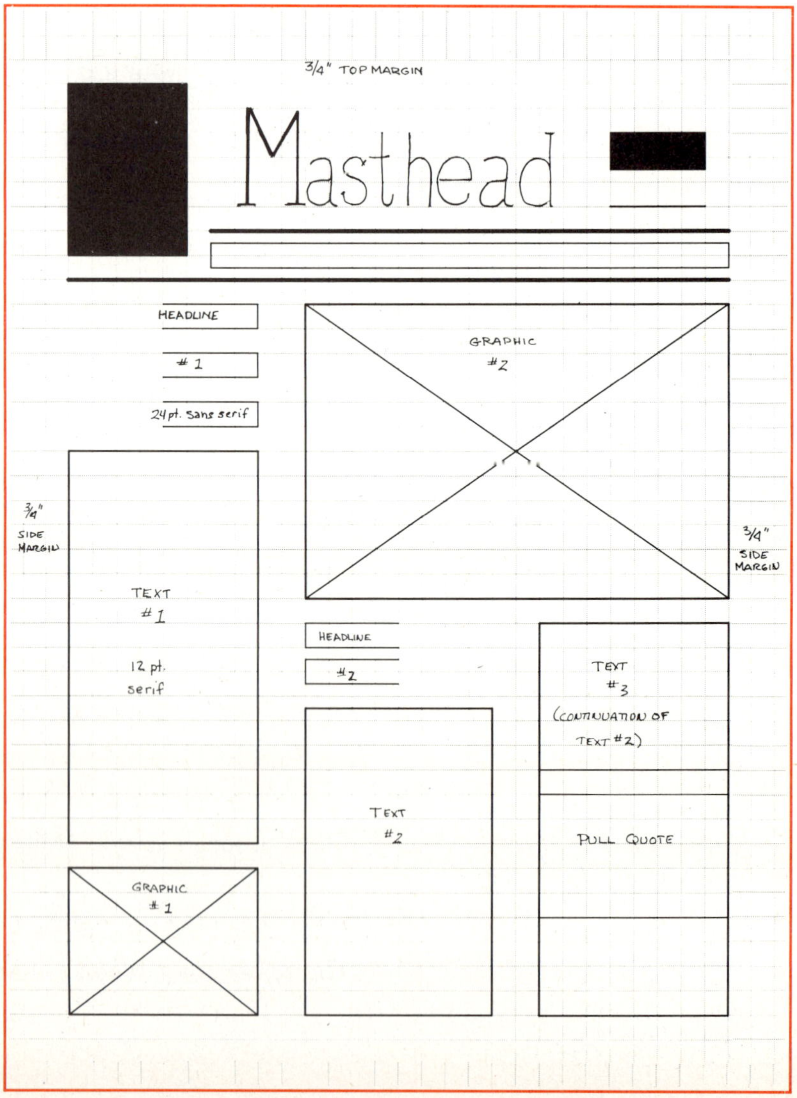

Figure 2.1 Rough Draft of the Page to be Assembled

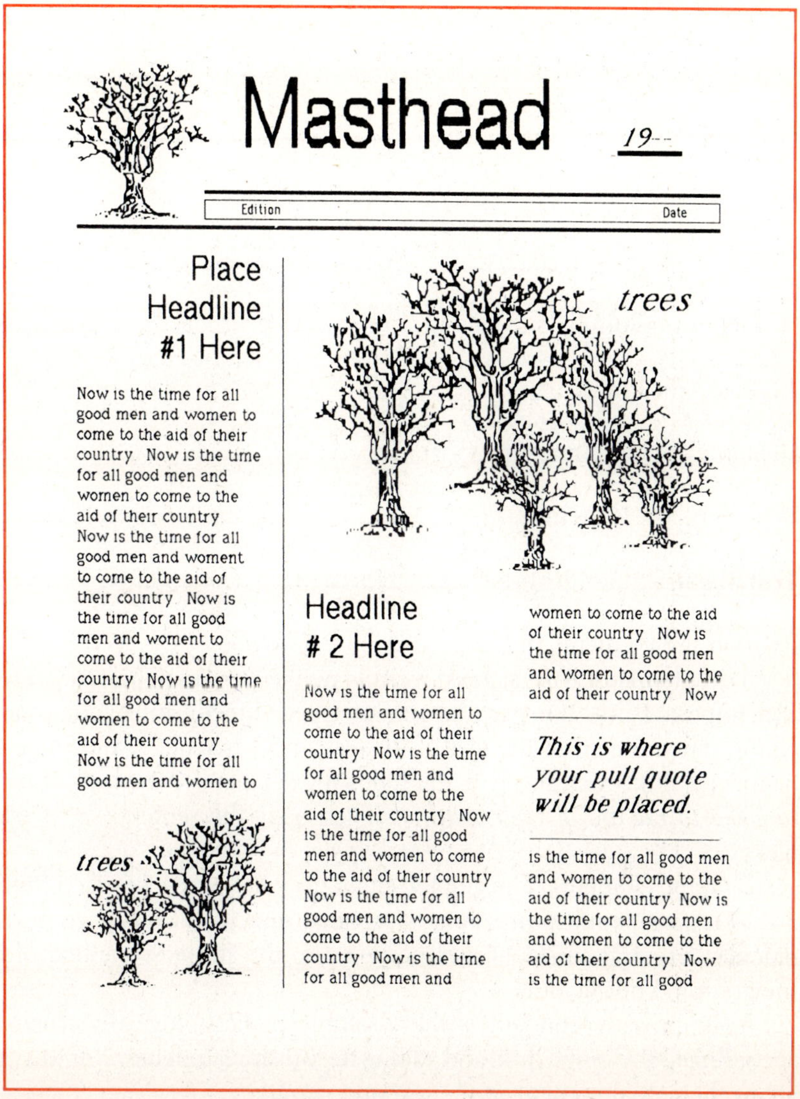

Masthead

19--

Edition Date

Place Headline #1 Here

Now is the time for all good men and women to come to the aid of their country. Now is the time for all good men and women to come to the aid of their country. Now is the time for all good men and woment to come to the aid of their country. Now is the time for all good men and woment to come to the aid of their country. Now is the time for all good men and women to come to the aid of their country. Now is the time for all good men and women to

trees

trees

Headline # 2 Here

Now is the time for all good men and women to come to the aid of their country. Now is the time for all good men and women to come to the aid of their country. Now is the time for all good men and women to come to the aid of their country. Now is the time for all good men and women to come to the aid of their country. Now is the time for all good men and

women to come to the aid of their country. Now is the time for all good men and women to come to the aid of their country. Now

This is where your pull quote will be placed.

is the time for all good men and women to come to the aid of their country. Now is the time for all good men and women to come to the aid of their country. Now is the time for all good

Figure 2.2 Printout of the Completed Publication

steps. You may also want to look at Figure 2.2, the actual printout of the publication. Once again, as the page size and margins are indicated in inches, convert to the appropriate measurements for your software, if necessary. Write the keystrokes and/or commands used to assemble the document. The answer will vary depending on your DTP software package. Indicate if a method is not available to you.

1. Using the rough sketch in Figure 2.1, develop a style sheet with the following page setup requirements. (Goal 1)

a. Page size = 8½ by 11 inches ____________________________________

b. Margins:

Top margin = ¾ inch ______

Bottom margin = ¾ inch ______

Side margins = ¾ inch ______

Gutter = ½ inch ______

c. Number of columns = 3, about 2 inches wide ______

d. Type specifications:

Headlines = 24 point sans serif ______

Body copy = 12 point serif ______

Text alignment = flush left ______

2. Position the elements in the page layout. (Goal 2)

Text elements: Text needed for this publication may be created using another software package and imported into the page layout, or typed directly into your page layout using your DTP text editor. The content of the text for this assembly practice is not important; feel free to develop your own copy. For example, type the following sentence: *Now is the time for all good men and women to come to the aid of their country.* Then copy the sentence as needed to create the required text blocks.

Graphic elements: The graphic elements you use can be taken from clip art files, created through a drawing or painting program, or created directly in the page layout. Since this is an assembly practice, exact graphics are not needed; use the simplest method of entering the required graphic images into your layout.

Your primary concern is the assembly process, logically placing the elements in the layout according to the rough draft and adding the finishing touches. For this practice, do NOT be concerned about the actual content of the text and graphic.

a. Begin by placing the masthead of your choice at the top of your page layout. You do not need to use the design in Figure 2.1. You may need to adjust the grid or baselines of your style sheet.

______

b. Type the first headline of your choice in the first column using the flush-right alignment.

______

c. Now place the text of your choice in the first column. With your software, you may need to enter text for all three columns first and then go back to add the graphics.

______

d. To complete the first column, place a graphic image at the bottom of the column. If necessary, adjust the text or graphic so both fit correctly within the first column.

______

e. Next place a second graphic into the layout. If necessary, resize the graphic image making it the same width as the second and third columns.

f. Type a second headline in the second column, using flush-left alignment.

g. Place the second section of text in the second column (the article should continue into the third column).

h. If the text did not completely fill the third column, enter the remaining text in the third column.

3. Edit, modify, or adjust the text and graphic elements to fit as indicated in Figures 2.1 and 2.2. Check all alignments. (Goal 3)

4. To improve the design of the page, add the following enhancements to the page layout. (Goal 4)

a. A vertical hairline between the first and second columns.

b. Create a pull quote in the middle of the text in the third column. Key any quote or phrase you want. Use an 18-point serif typeface with italic type style, set the pull quote off with a rule above and below the quote, then adjust the body copy accordingly.

c. Try placing a border around the first graphic image. Decide whether you like the design better with or without the border.

5. Accept the design as final. (Goal 5)

6. Using the filename *SAMPLE*, save your file to your own formatted data disk. (Goal 6)

7. An advantage of DTP software is the ease with which you can make changes in a layout. Since your file is saved to the disk, try experimenting and generate an alternative design. Save your alternative design as *SAMPLE2*. (Goal 6)

COACH'S CORNER

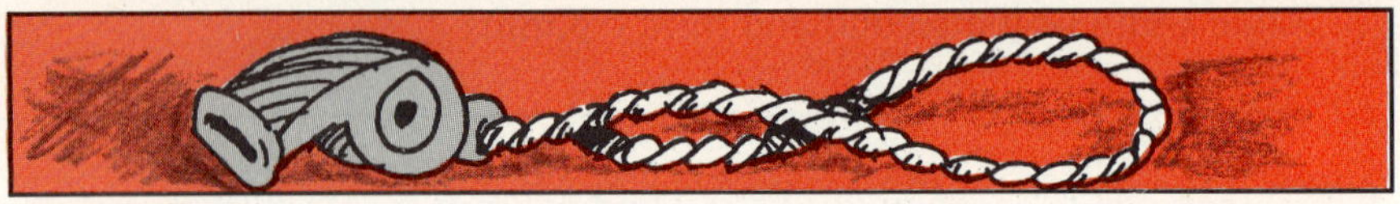

This tryout session can be considered a test of your endurance. Did you make it to the finish line by assembling your first document according to the rules (the Figure 2.1 rough draft sketch)? This is what DTP is all about—designing and then assembling publications. The skill of building effective publications is developed through lots of practice. To begin, keep your design simple and do not try to include every trick you have learned in one document. During your next tryout session you will have the opportunity to print the document you just assembled.

PLAYER'S NOTES:

CLASS HOUR: ______ DATE: ______ NAME: ____________

TRYOUT SESSION 6

Printing a Document

Printing refers to producing a hard copy of your completed page or pages. Items to consider in connection with printing are the quality of resolution desired (dots per inch), the number of copies needed, and the size of the document. Often a draft-quality copy printed on a dot-matrix printer is used as a last check for errors. Then a laser printer is used to produce the final copies of the publication or a camera-ready master.

TERMINOLOGY

The following terms relate to printing a document. Be sure to review the words before you begin to print.

Camera-Ready — The final copy of a publication used to produce the negative for a printing plate.

Dot-Matrix Printer — An impact line printer; the images are printed by striking the paper with print pins through an inked ribbon.

Draft Quality — The dry-run printing of a publication with a dot-matrix printer, not of reproduction quality. This usually prints faster than higher quality methods.

Hard Copy — A printed copy of the page layout.

Laser Printer — A printer that shows images transferred by laser beam on xerographic drum to paper, like a photocopier. This is usually a better quality printer than a dot-matrix printer.

Reproduction Quality — High-quality printing of a publication done with a laser printer.

TRYOUT SESSION GOALS

Now read the following goals and complete the tryout session where you will print the document created and saved in Tryout Session 5.

1. Retrieving a saved file.
2. Printing the document in draft quality.
3. Printing the document in reproduction quality.
4. Creating a print file of the document on the disk.

TRYOUT SESSION

To begin this tryout session, recall the file (*SAMPLE*) containing your document. Then complete each of the following steps. Write the keystrokes and/or commands you use to print your document. The answers will vary depending on your DTP software. Indicate if the printing option is not available to you.

1. Retrieve your file called *SAMPLE*. (Goal 1)

   ____

2. Print a draft-quality copy of your document. (Goal 2)

   ____

a. Proofread your hard copy for typographical errors. Make needed corrections in spelling, punctuation, hyphenation, or justification.

b. Review your hard copy for technique errors. Make adjustments in consistency in spacing or type specifications, proper use of graphics, or enhancements.

c. Review your hard copy by checking the design elements. Make changes in the overall appearance, balance, effective use of white space, etc.

3. Now that all needed corrections are made, print a reproduction quality or camera-ready copy of your document. This may take some time, so be patient! (Goal 3)

   ____

4. Finally, create a print file of your document on your disk, which can be sent to a typsetting machine. (Goal 4)

   ____

COACH'S CORNER

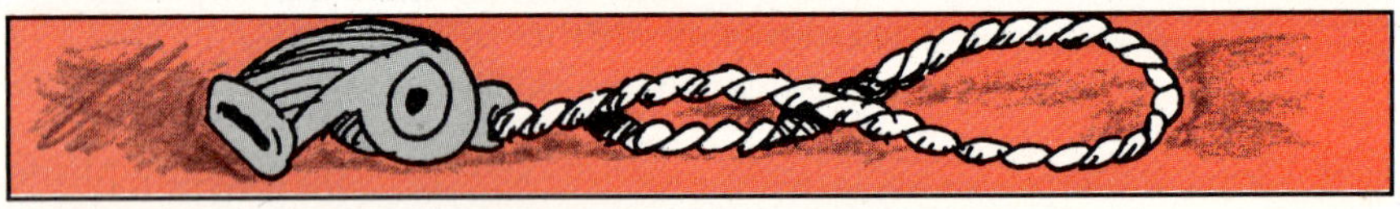

This was an easy practice today—printing a document! Were you pleased with your printout? Now that you have progressed through all the tryout sessions relating to operating your desktop publisher, your focus will turn to what is actually the first step in the DTP cycle, preplanning your document. Your last tryout session explains how to develop the game plan. Remember: Without a plan, your document is doomed to a sudden death!

CLASS HOUR: ______ DATE: ______ NAME: ____________

TRYOUT SESSION 7
Preplanning Your Document

Designing a publication does not just happen; it requires planning from the very beginning. Before you actually create a document at the computer using desktop publishing software, you need to go through a **preplanning process**. This process involves answering questions relating to the document you are about to develop, questions about publication requirements, characteristics of the desired audience, message content, and how the needed graphic and text elements will be developed.

Note that this topic on "preplanning" is being discussed at the end of Part 2. You have become more familiar with your DTP software in the first six tryout sessions. It is time to stop and take a look at how far you've gone!

TERMINOLOGY

Now that you are familiar with the terms relating to page setup, graphics, text, assembling, and printing, your next step will be putting it all together to develop publications. The following definition is repeated for emphasis.

Desktop Publishing — The process of planning and creating computer-generated publications containing graphics and text that appear to have been professionally printed.

TRYOUT SESSION GOALS

Now read the following goals and review the list of questions in the tryout session.

1. Examining the publication requirements.
2. Understanding the characteristics of the desired audience.
3. Determining the message content for the publication.
4. Deciding how the graphics and text elements will be developed.

TRYOUT SESSION

To begin this tryout session, read the following questions. They are presented only as a guide, as you should develop your own list of specific questions relating to individual projects. Remember: Before you begin to design a publication, you need a plan as to what you want to accomplish.

1. Note the following questions relating to the publication requirements. (Goal 1)

a. What is the purpose of the publication?

b. What type of publication are you creating?

c. What page size and shape will be used?

d. How will the publication be distributed?

e. Are competitive materials available?

f. What are the distribution deadlines?

g. What are the budget guidelines?

2. Note the following questions relating to characteristics of the desired audience. (Goal 2)

a. Who is your reader?

b. How will you attract your reader?

c. When and where will the message be read?

d. What is the attention span and motivation of the reader?

e. Will the publication be required or leisure reading?

f. What action will be expected from the reader?

3. Note the following questions relating to the message content. (Goal 3)

a. What type of information are you communicating?

b. Is the content aimed toward the reader?

c. In what direction is the message taking the reader?

d. Is an appropriate business image created?

e. What is the most important or significant point?

f. Is the purpose of the publication expressed?

4. Note the following questions relating to the development of graphics and text elements. (Goal 4)

a. What graphic images will be needed?

b. Will clip art files be used? If so, which ones?

c. Will graphic images be created in a painting or drawing program?

d. Who is responsible for developing the graphic images?

e. Will the text files be created on a word processor?

f. Who is responsible for developing the text files?

g. Will the text be keyed directly into the layout?

COACH'S CORNER

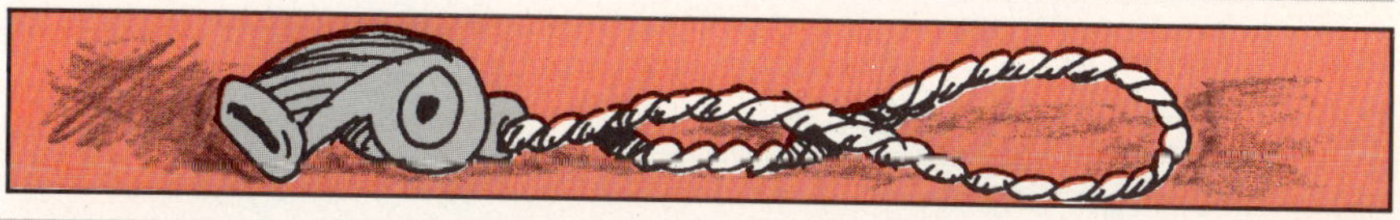

The buzzer signals the end of our tryout sessions for the DTP team. After completing the seven rounds of exercises, you should be familiar with the strengths and weaknesses of your particular desktop publishing software. Also, you will be aware of areas where you could use additional workout time yourself.

ANNOUNCEMENT: Anyone who made it to this point—successfully completing all the tryout sessions—has been selected for the DTP team. Congratulations on making the team! Your first practice will start shortly.

PLAYER'S NOTES:

CLASS HOUR: ______ DATE: ______ NAME: ____________________

THE *Game Fundamentals* QUIZ

Directions: Complete the following statements and answer the questions.

1. Is a page size of 8½ by 11 inches considered a landscape or portrait layout orientation?

   ____

2. List two changes that can be made to clip art that is already in a page layout.

   a. ____

   b. ____

3. Can text be typed directly into a page layout? Yes or no. ______________

4. Eliminating the unwanted area of a graphic image is called ______________.

5. When doing your preplanning, what are two characteristics you should know about your audience?

   a. ____

   b. ____

6. DTP is the abbreviation for ______________________.

7. A ______________ printer is used to produce a draft-quality copy of the publication.

8. Once a line of text is placed in a layout, can it be changed? Yes or no. ______________

9. List the four ways text can be aligned in a layout.

   a. ____

   b. ____

   c. ____

   d. ____

10. Explain the difference between a serif and sans serif typeface.

    ____

    ____

11. One inch is equal to ______________ picas.

12. What are two graphic drawing tools?

a. ______________________________

b. ______________________________

13. Define *hard copy*.

____

____

14. Should the purpose of a publication be known before you begin to design the layout? Yes or no.

____

15. Adjusting the appearance of text to follow the shape of an encountered graphic is called

______________________________.

PART 3 The Practice Drills

OBJECTIVES

1. To design and create letterhead stationery.
2. To design and create flyers for different purposes.
3. To design and create specialty DTP items for different situations.
4. To design and create specific business forms.

INTRODUCTION

Welcome to the DTP team! Your tryout sessions were successful and now it's on to the practice camp. Listen while one of the seasoned veterans talks about the practice drills, so you will know what to expect.

First, develop the correct practice routine of following the DTP cycle (planning, designing, assembling, and printing) for each drill. Your workout will begin with simple drills (letterheads). Then you'll progress through a variety of increasingly difficult drills (flyers and speciality items). Finally, toward the end of practice camp, you'll tackle the complex drills (business forms). Plenty of exercises are available to provide as much practice as you (or the Coach) feel is required to master each technique. To guide you in developing your skills, each drill is set up as follows:

1. States a *Practice Goal to Accomplish* by describing the type of document to be designed and created.
2. Suggests *Strategies to Consider* by pointing out some basic design principles related to creating an effective document.
3. Provides *Supplies to Use* in the form of suggested information to be contained in the document.
4. Shows a *Chart to Follow* by presenting a thumbnail sketch that can be your guide for designing the document.

These practice drills may be a little tough, but this is a normal part of learning a skill. To reach your potential and perfect your skills takes dedication, which means practicing techniques over and over.

GUIDELINES FOR LETTERHEADS

A **letterhead** is the printed design on stationery that normally includes the name, address, and phone number. For businesses, a company name is used. If a company logo is available, it may be included as part of the letterhead design. A **logo** is a design created to identify or represent a specific company or idea. See Figure 3.1. Optional items to include in a letterhead might be a slogan, company philosophy, or the names and titles of individuals in the firm.

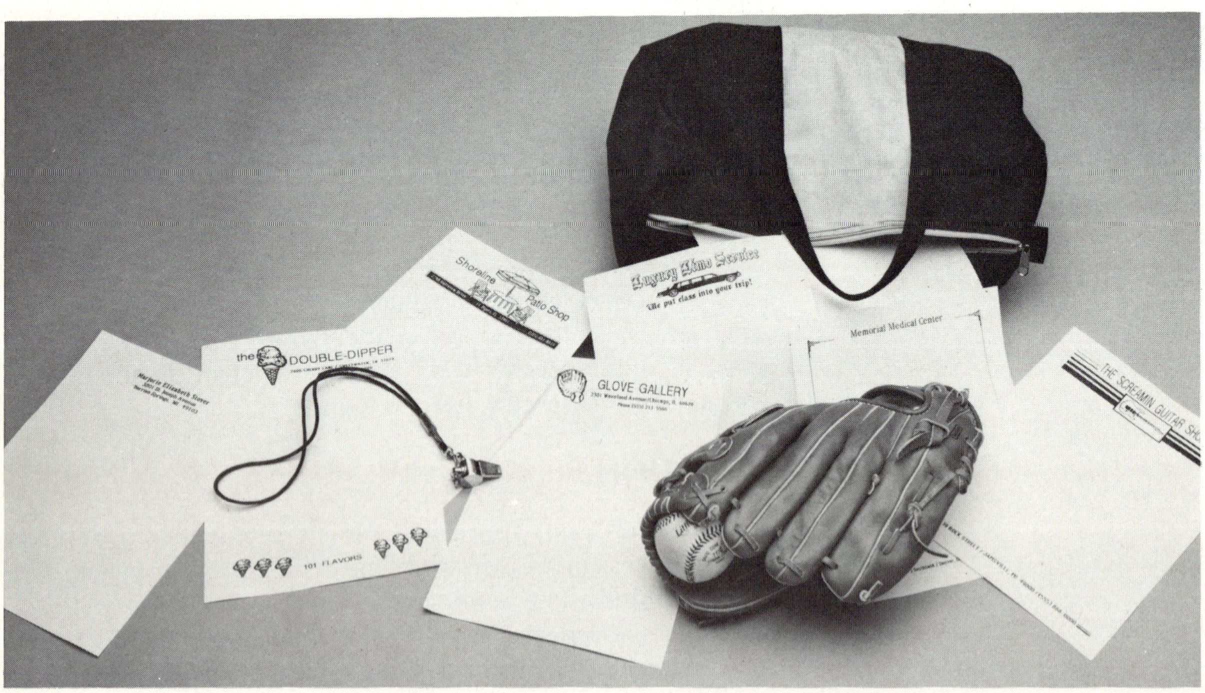

Figure 3.1 A logo is a design created to identify or represent a specific company or idea.

POINTS TO CONSIDER

Note the following considerations as you design your letterheads:

1. The standard paper size for business stationery is 8½ by 11 inches.
2. The purpose of the letterhead is to communicate company information in an appealing manner, not to decorate the page.
3. Usually the letterhead, or at least the main part of the design, is located at the top of the stationery.
4. The letterhead design should be distinct from the message area and not detract from the message.
5. A visual image of a business can be established by the design of the letterhead.
6. The typical height for a letterhead is 2 to 2½ inches, which includes the top margin and the design. If part of the design appears at the bottom of the page, keep this information within a height of 1½ inches.
7. Some businesses use a reduced version or portion of the letterhead design on their business envelopes, note paper, business cards, etc.

COACH'S CORNER

Nervous about your first practice? Don't be, you will do just fine. The first series of drills should be rather easy, as you design letterhead stationery for various companies. Remember, the practices are designed as just that: P-R-A-C-T-I-C-E! Use this opportunity to start building your strength in the areas of DTP design by paying close attention to the strategies as they are presented.

Well, are you ready to develop those DTP skills? Okay, grab your gear and head to the practice field!

CLASS HOUR: ______ DATE: ______ NAME: ______________________

PRACTICE DRILL A-1

Create a Letterhead

PRACTICE GOAL TO ACCOMPLISH

Using text only, select one typeface and design the letterhead for an individual to use as personal stationery.

STRATEGIES TO CONSIDER

Before creating your letterhead, note the following suggestions for some basic design hints:

1. Try blending the different type styles (bold, italics) and type sizes (10, 12, 18, 24, or 36 points) until an appropriate combination is found for the information. (COACH'S TIP: Remember, the name is the most important item in the letterhead. Therefore it is the dominant element on the page and should be keyed in either a bold typeface and/or the largest type size.)
2. Although normally the letterhead text is centered at the top of the stationery, you can try positioning it elsewhere. You may create an interesting design by experimenting.
3. A letterhead for an individual does not necessarily include a phone number, but one can be included in this drill.

SUPPLIES TO USE

The following information should appear on your letterhead design. Add the name, street address, city, state, and ZIP Code. The use of the phone number is optional. If you like, create a letterhead using your own name and address instead.

NAME OF INDIVIDUAL: *Marjorie Elizabeth Stover*

ADDRESS: *3801 St. Joseph Avenue, Berrien Springs, MI 49103*

PHONE: *(555) 471-7353 (optional)*

CHART TO FOLLOW

Use the following thumbnail sketch as a suggested layout for your letterhead design. Be sure to use an appropriate file name for your document. Save your file on your own formatted data disk. Print a copy of your final letterhead. **In the remainder of this text-workbook, you will not be told to save or print a file.** You are expected to know when to do this to complete the exercise.

Marjorie Elizabeth Stover
3801 St Joseph Avenue
Berrien Springs, MI 49103

PLAYER'S NOTES:

CLASS HOUR: ______ DATE: ______ NAME: ______________________

PRACTICE DRILL A-2

Create a Letterhead

PRACTICE GOAL TO ACCOMPLISH

Select two typefaces as you design the letterhead for a professional firm using text only. A list of three or more people associated with the firm should be included in the design.

STRATEGIES TO CONSIDER

Before creating your letterhead, note the following suggestions for some basic design hints:

1. When using two typefaces, be sure they complement each other.
2. Because the typeface itself can portray an image of the business, select a typeface that denotes professionalism in keeping with the nature of the firm.
3. Try placing the list of names in different locations on the page until a balanced design is reached.
4. When deciding where the list should appear, consider how easy it would be to add or delete a name in updating the list.

SUPPLIES TO USE

The following information should appear on your letterhead design. Add the name, street address, city, state, ZIP Code, and phone numbers. Also add the list of person's names. If you like, use your own data for the firm of your choice.

NAME OF FIRM: *Johnson & Johnson Attorneys*

ADDRESS: *300 The Black Building, 2002 South Washington Avenue, Woodberry Forest, Virginia 22989*

PHONE: *(555) 344-6000 and (555) 344-6100*

PEOPLE: *Allen T. Johnson, Robert A. Johnson, Kenneth C. Hernandez, and Josefina M. Garcia*

CHART TO FOLLOW

Use the following thumbnail sketch as a suggested layout for your letterhead design.

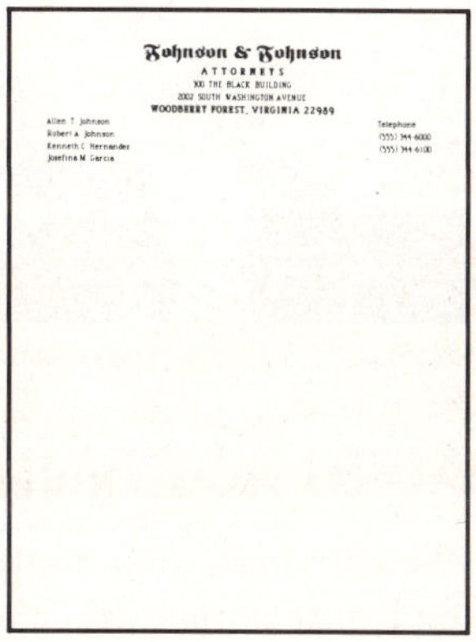

PLAYER'S NOTES:

CLASS HOUR: ______ DATE: ______ NAME: ____________________________

PRACTICE DRILL A-3

Create a Letterhead

PRACTICE GOAL TO ACCOMPLISH

Now you will design the letterhead for a sports-affiliated business. This time the design should include text along with an appropriate graphic image that pertains to the business.

STRATEGIES TO CONSIDER

Before creating your letterhead, note the following suggestions for some basic design hints:

1. Often a logo designed specifically for a company or a related graphic image will be used along with the business name because it provides instant company identification to the reader.
2. When determining the size to make a graphic image, remember the business name is normally the most important element and should be the dominant element on the page.
3. Balance must be considered when combining text with a graphic image. Try placing the elements in different locations on the page until you understand how the concept of balance works.

SUPPLIES TO USE

The following information should appear on your letterhead design. If you like, you can use the data and logo of a different business.

NAME OF BUSINESS: *The Glove Gallery*

ADDRESS: *2301 Waveland Avenue, Chicago, IL 60620*

PHONE: *(555) 213-5566*

GRAPHIC IMAGE: *A baseball mitt or any other image that implies sports*

CHART TO FOLLOW

Use the following thumbnail sketch as a suggested layout for your letterhead design.

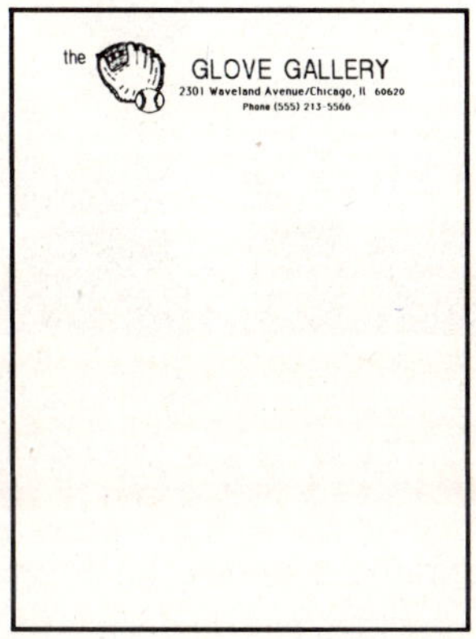

PLAYER'S NOTES:

CLASS HOUR: ______ DATE: ______ NAME: ____________________

PRACTICE DRILL A-4

Create a Letterhead

PRACTICE GOAL TO ACCOMPLISH

Use a display or decorative typeface for the name of the business. Include an appropriate company logo as you design the letterhead for an auto-related business.

STRATEGIES TO CONSIDER

Before creating your letterhead, note the following suggestions for some basic design hints:

1. Experiment with several display or decorative typefaces. Remember to keep the tone of the overall design businesslike. (COACH'S TIP: A special typeface must have a purpose and should be used sparingly.)
2. The graphic image should play a secondary role in your design. This can be accomplished by keeping the size small and/or locating it on the page so it does not detract from the special type.
3. Take care when combining different types of elements on a page; they should produce a unified design.
4. Try putting the address and phone number at the bottom of the page for a change.

SUPPLIES TO USE

The following information should appear on your letterhead design. If you like, you can use the data and logo of a different business.

NAME OF BUSINESS: *Luxury Limo Service*

ADDRESS: *5005 Short Drive, New York, NY 10001*

PHONE: *(555) 212-2909*

SLOGAN: *We put class into your trip!*

GRAPHIC IMAGE: *A limousine or other automobile image*

CHART TO FOLLOW

Use the following thumbnail sketch as a suggested layout for your letterhead design.

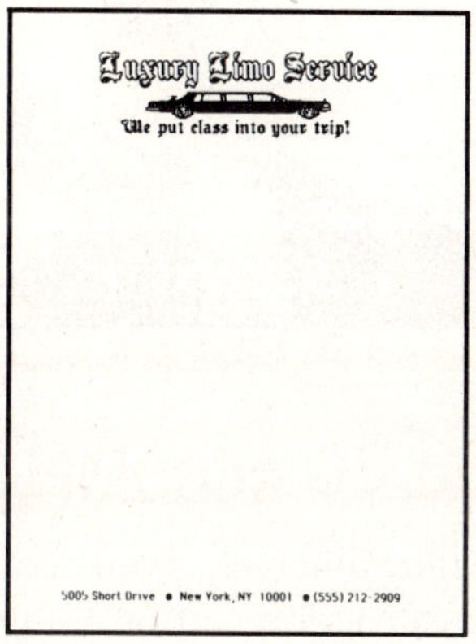

PLAYER'S NOTES:

CLASS HOUR: ______ DATE: ______ NAME: ____________________

PRACTICE DRILL A-5

Create a Letterhead

PRACTICE GOAL TO ACCOMPLISH

Let's try something a little different as you design the letterhead for a medical business. See how creative you can be using a border as part of the total design.

STRATEGIES TO CONSIDER

Before creating your letterhead, note the following suggestions for some basic design hints:

1. Keep the border simple and light rather than bold. It should not overpower the page and detract from the company name, which should be the focal element of the design.
2. A border in your design is a method of setting off the message area of the letter.
3. Incorporating the text with the border can produce a unified design for the letterhead.
4. You can either use a piece of clip art or draw your own border. You can also piece together sections of a clip art border to make a complete border.

SUPPLIES TO USE

The following information should appear on your letterhead design. If you like, you can use the data of a different business. Use a different border if desired.

NAME OF BUSINESS: *Memorial Medical Center*

ADDRESS: *7675 Southfield, Denver, CO 80200*

PHONE: *(555) 259-7042*

GRAPHIC IMAGE: *A simple border—drawn or clip art*

CHART TO FOLLOW

Use the following thumbnail sketch as a suggested layout for your letterhead design.

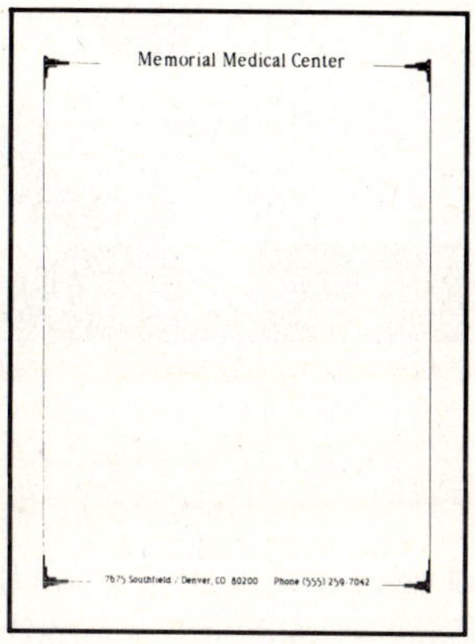

PLAYER'S NOTES:

CLASS HOUR: ______ DATE: ______ NAME: ______________________

PRACTICE DRILL A-6

Create a Letterhead

PRACTICE GOAL TO ACCOMPLISH

Design the letterhead for a music store. Use the line and box tools to create your own graphic image as part of the letterhead design.

STRATEGIES TO CONSIDER

Before creating your letterhead, note the following suggestions for some basic design hints:

1. For it to be effective, keep your design relatively simple. (COACH'S TIP: It is helpful to sketch your idea for the GRAPHIC IMAGE on a sheet of paper before you actually begin to create it at the computer.)
2. As you create the design, use lines and boxes with the same point size and then experiment with various point sizes until you find the exact combination desired.
3. A box or border can be used to set off graphics. So, for an added dimension, try combining a graphic image within your design.

SUPPLIES TO USE

The following information should appear on your letterhead design. If you like, you can use the data and graphics for a different business.

NAME OF BUSINESS: *The Screamin Guitar Shop*

ADDRESS: *209 Rock Street, Jamsville, MI 49000*

PHONE: *(555) 888-0000*

GRAPHIC IMAGE: *An electric guitar or other appropriate musical instrument*

CHART TO FOLLOW

Use the following thumbnail sketch as a suggested layout for your letterhead design.

PLAYER'S NOTES:

CLASS HOUR: ______ DATE: ______ NAME: ____________________

PRACTICE DRILL A-7

Create a Letterhead

PRACTICE GOAL TO ACCOMPLISH

Using the technique of reversed type, design the letterhead for a furniture-related store. The use of reversed type should be approached with caution.

STRATEGIES TO CONSIDER

Before creating your letterhead, note the following suggestions for some basic design hints:

1. Reversed type should be considered an element of emphasis; use it sparingly.
2. Since reversed type is generally more difficult to read than regular type, be sure to select a large type size and/or a bold type style that will enhance readability of the text. (COACH'S TIP: Sometimes text must be entered as graphics to allow reversing.)
3. A sans serif typeface is easier to read reversed because it does not contain the fine cross-lines on the characters.

SUPPLIES TO USE

The following information should appear on your letterhead design. If you like, you can use the data and graphics of a different business.

NAME OF BUSINESS: *Shoreline Patio Shop*

ADDRESS: *2298 Gulfview Drive, Ft. Myers, FL 33901*

PHONE: *(555) 481-8811*

GRAPHIC IMAGE: *Patio furniture or a graphic that implies furniture or a patio*

CHART TO FOLLOW

Use the following thumbnail sketch as a suggested layout for your letterhead design.

PLAYER'S NOTES:

CLASS HOUR: ______ DATE: ______ NAME: ____________________

PRACTICE DRILL A-8

Create a Letterhead

PRACTICE GOAL TO ACCOMPLISH

The last letterhead you will design is for an eating establishment. Select a graphic image that can be resized, flipped, and duplicated in different locations of the design.

STRATEGIES TO CONSIDER

Before creating your letterhead, note the following suggestions for some basic design hints:

1. Select a graphic image that logically can appear more than once to create an effective design.
2. Flipping some graphic images makes them unrealistic. However, when an image appears on different sides of a page, often it must be flipped to face the correct direction. (COACH'S TIP: How the reader views a page can be guided by the direction a graphic image faces. Keep your reader on the page!)
3. The size of a graphic image plays an important role in the total concept being designed, especially when duplicating the image. Be sure you create a design and do not just place additional graphic images on the page.

SUPPLIES TO USE

The following information should appear on your letterhead design. If you like, you can use the data and graphics of a different business.

NAME OF BUSINESS: *The Double-Dipper*

ADDRESS: *7006 Cherry Lane, Sweetwater, TN 37874*

PHONE: *(555) 429-6000*

SLOGAN: *101 Flavors*

GRAPHIC IMAGE: *Double-dip ice cream cone, or other ice cream or food graphic image. Make sure you can tell that the selected image is reversed.*

CHART TO FOLLOW

Use the following thumbnail sketch as a suggested layout for your letterhead design.

PLAYER'S NOTES:

CLASS HOUR: ________ DATE: ________ NAME: ____________________

PRACTICE DRILL A-9

Create a Letterhead

PRACTICE GOAL TO ACCOMPLISH

As a final drill in this section, you will design an envelope and business card using the information from two previous drills. Use the letterhead you designed in Drill A-8 to create an envelope that will coordinate with the stationery. Then develop a business card for one of the people from Drill A-2.

STRATEGIES TO CONSIDER

Before creating your envelope and business card, note the following suggestions for some basic design hints:

1. Using the entire letterhead design in a reduced version depends on whether the design lends itself to an exact reduction. Some of the detail can get lost.
2. To reduce the logo, you will need to select and copy the logo to a smaller size. Then use this in a different file for your envelope and card. You should save your logo as a separate file for convenience.
3. Be sure the company identity developed with the letterhead is carried over when using the information in other places.
4. You may need to recreate the logo if you cannot copy between files in your software. You could save two versions of the same file and edit the second file for the envelope and card.
5. Include only pertinent information on business cards because space is limited. The company name continues to be a dominant element—not the person's name.
6. Normally a smaller type size is used on envelopes and business cards due to their size.
7. The logo design on the envelope should start about ¼ inch from the trim. On the business card, your type and graphics should be no less than ⅛ inch from the trim.

SUPPLIES TO USE

The following dimensions should be used for your envelope and business card design. Use the data from Drill A-8 for the envelope. Use the data from Drill A-2 for the business card. If you like, you can use data and graphics from different businesses.

SIZE OF ENVELOPE: *4⅛ by 9½ inches*

SIZE OF BUSINESS CARD: *3½ by 2 inches*

CHART TO FOLLOW

Use the following thumbnail sketches as suggested layouts for your envelope and business card designs. To complete the envelope, you may be able to draw only a partial border to suggest the outline of the envelope. You could also rotate the image to fit on a complete 4⅛- by 9½-inch envelope border. For the business card, draw a border to suggest the size of the card.

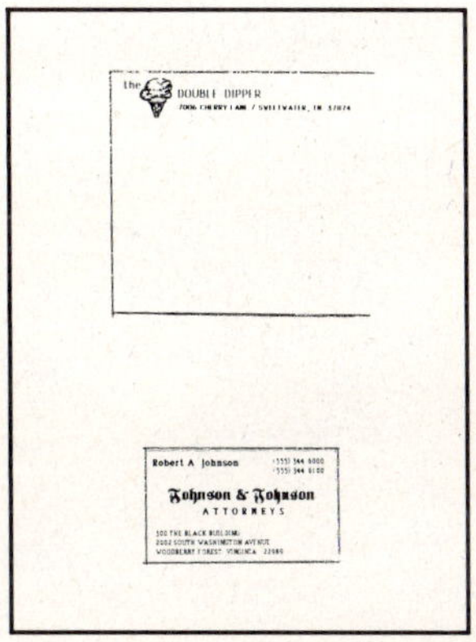

PLAYER'S NOTES:

GUIDELINES FOR FLYERS

Flyers are promotional posters used for various purposes. They provide information that announces upcoming events, advertises sales or business ventures, promotes special services, highlights activities, provides directions, or numerous other possibilities. Refer to Figure 3.2. Flyers are also called notices, bills, posters, or announcements.

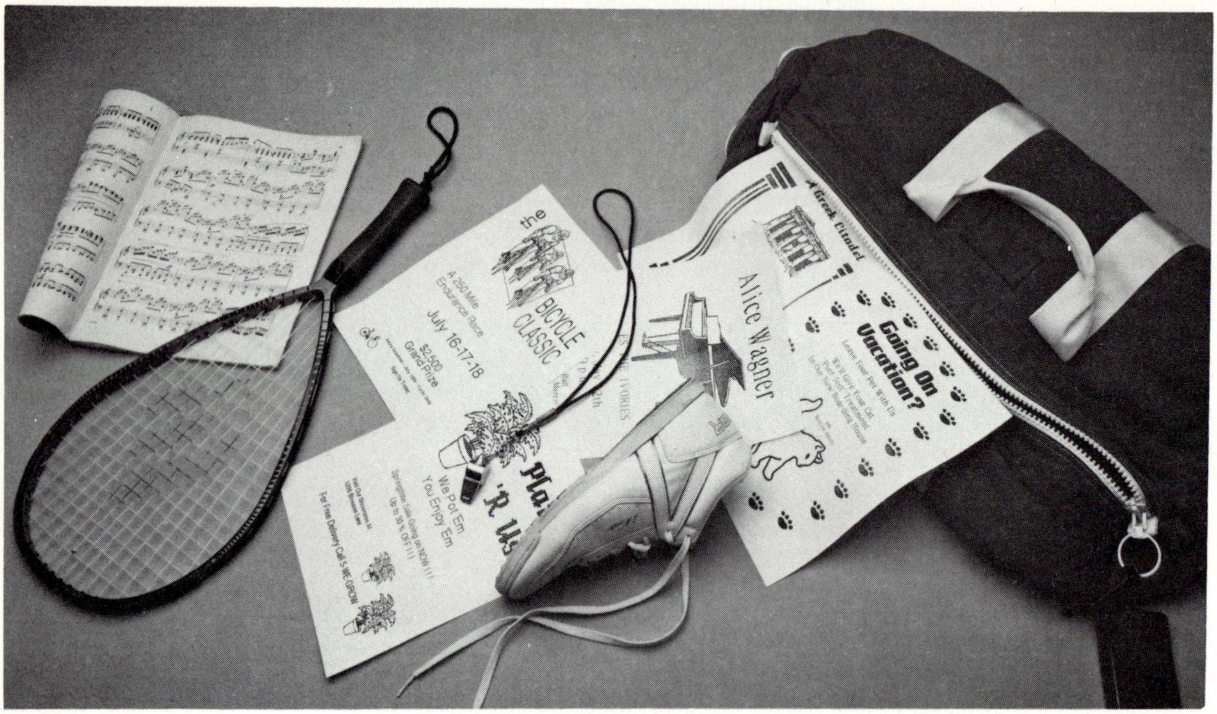

Figure 3.2 Flyers provide information that announces, promotes, and advertises anything you want.

POINTS TO CONSIDER

Note these following considerations as you design your flyers:

1. The objective of a flyer is to capture the reader's attention.
2. Keep text to a minimum, yet provide enough information for the reader to take the desired action.
3. Display, decorative, or large typefaces are excellent for flyers.
4. More than one typeface is often used. However, do not use more than three typefaces per flyer.
5. Flyers tend to contain more graphics than other publications.
6. The graphic image is often the main element of a flyer. Using a dominant graphic image in the design is often better than cluttering the flyer with numerous small graphics.
7. Keep the design simple and to the point. Do not overdo it with many different design elements.

8. A size often used for flyers is the standard page size of 8½ by 11 inches. This is convenient and economical for duplication.
9. A flyer is normally not required reading, so visual appeal is important.

COACH'S CORNER

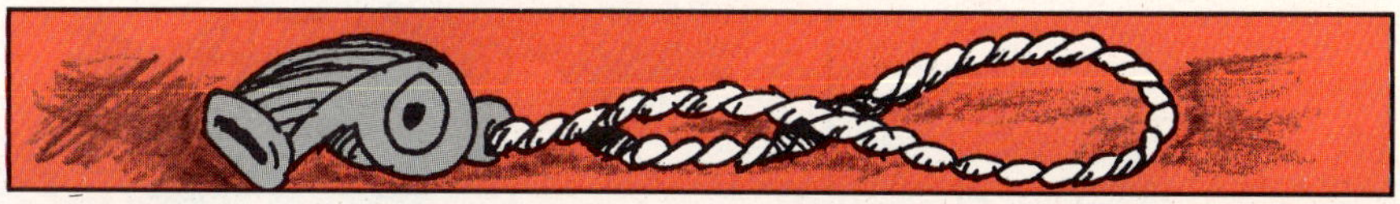

Your practice with letterheads provided a warmup for the training that will take place throughout practice camp. As your attention turns to the area of flyers, you will continue designing routine types of publications in an effort to master the basic techniques involved. Remember the old adage: *Practice makes perfect*. Also notice that the strategies have identified several "unwritten rules" you should consider as you concentrate on perfecting your DTP skills.

CLASS HOUR: ______ DATE: ______ NAME: ____________________

PRACTICE DRILL B-1

Create a Flyer

PRACTICE GOAL TO ACCOMPLISH

To begin, design a flyer that promotes a musical concert or related activity scheduled to take place in the near future. Keep your first flyer simple by using one typeface and one graphic image.

STRATEGIES TO CONSIDER

Before creating your flyer, note the following suggestions for some basic design hints:

1. When working with one typeface, remember to vary the type sizes and/or type styles to highlight the specific points. The type size is directly related to the importance of the information.
2. All capital letters will make the text appear larger. (COACH'S TIP: Text typed in all capital letters can be difficult to read.)
3. A large graphic image can grab the reader's attention and provide instant recognition as to message content.

SUPPLIES TO USE

The following information should appear on your flyer design. If you like, you can create a flyer using the data and graphic image for the event of your choice.

MESSAGE: *Alice Wagner Tickles The Ivories*

DATE: *Friday, May 12th*

TIME: *8:00 p.m.*

LOCATION: *Concert Hall, 1001 Music Alley, Merriville*

GRAPHIC IMAGE: *A grand piano, upright piano, or other musical keyboard image*

CHART TO FOLLOW

Use the following thumbnail sketch as a suggested layout for your flyer design.

PLAYER'S NOTES:

CLASS HOUR: ______ DATE: ______ NAME: ______________________

PRACTICE DRILL B-2

Create a Flyer

PRACTICE GOAL TO ACCOMPLISH

Now design a flyer announcing an upcoming event or contest that will motivate the reader to participate in the activity. Once again, use only one typeface, but include a couple of graphic images in your design.

STRATEGIES TO CONSIDER

Before creating your flyer, note the following suggestions for some basic design hints:

1. To create a special effect with the text, try rotating a word or displaying a word vertically. Use caution with this technique; you can easily lose your reader if the message is difficult to read.
2. A sans serif typeface in a large type size tends to attract the reader's eye if the copy is short.
3. Use one dominant graphic image along with smaller related graphics. But do not clutter the page.
4. Be sure to identify the action your reader needs to take in order to participate.

SUPPLIES TO USE

The following information should appear on your flyer design. If you like, you can use the data and graphic for a different event.

MESSAGE: *The Bicycle Classic, A 250 Mile Endurance Race with a $2,500 Grand Prize*

ACTION DESIRED: *Entry Deadline—July 10th—Cycle Shoppe, Sign Up Today*

DATE: *July 16, 17, & 18*

GRAPHIC IMAGE: *A bicycle or other appropriate sports graphic*

CHART TO FOLLOW

Use the following thumbnail sketch as a suggested layout for your flyer design.

PLAYER'S NOTES:

CLASS HOUR: ______ DATE: ______ NAME: ______________________________

PRACTICE DRILL B-3

Create a Flyer

PRACTICE GOAL TO ACCOMPLISH

This time you will design a flyer that advertises a sale being held at a retail store. Use more than one typeface along with the same graphic image in different sizes.

STRATEGIES TO CONSIDER

Before creating your flyer, note the following suggestions for some basic design hints:

1. Select the desired typefaces with care; be sure they blend with one another. (COACH'S TIP: Too many typefaces on one page tends to confuse the reader. Remember, a rule of thumb says never more than three per page.)
2. Be selective with the graphic images you use. They should enhance the message plus attract attention.
3. Keep the design simple and informative. It is the message you want your reader to notice.

SUPPLIES TO USE

The following information should appear on your flyer design. If you like, use the data and graphic from a different business.

BUSINESS: *Plants 'R Us*

ADDRESS: *1200 Blossom Lane*

MESSAGE: *We Pot 'Em, You Enjoy 'Em*
Springtime Sale Going On NOW!!! Up to 30% OFF!!!

ACTION: *Visit Our Showroom*
For Free Delivery Call 5-WE-GROW

GRAPHIC IMAGE: *A plant of some kind that can be easily copied in different sizes*

CHART TO FOLLOW

Use the following thumbnail sketch as a suggested layout for your flyer design.

PLAYER'S NOTES:

CLASS HOUR: ______ DATE: ______ NAME: ______________________

PRACTICE DRILL B-4
Create a Flyer

PRACTICE GOAL TO ACCOMPLISH

Design a flyer to post in the reception area of a business that highlights a new service available to clients. Use a border around the outside of your flyer to enclose the message.

STRATEGIES TO CONSIDER

Before creating your flyer, note the following suggestions for some basic design hints:

1. You may wish to create your own border by using a graphic image that relates to the message and can be repeated in a pattern. For example, in this drill, a paw print is used for the cat image.
2. The border should tie the elements together rather than overpower or distract from the message by merely decorating the page.
3. A friendly typeface helps your flyer appeal to the desired clients. (COACH'S TIP: A serif typeface is considered friendlier than a sans serif typeface because the cross-lines tend to guide the reader's eye through the message.)
4. Avoid clutter; do not fill the page completely with text and graphic. White space is needed to give the reader's eye a rest.

SUPPLIES TO USE

The following information should appear on your flyer design. If you like, use the data and graphic from a different business.

MESSAGE: *Going On Vacation? Leave Your Pet With Us. We'll Give Your Cat "Purr-fect" Treatment In Our New Boarding House.*

ACTION: *Ask Nicol for details*

GRAPHIC IMAGE: *A cat and/or a paw print or other appropriate animal image*

CHART TO FOLLOW

Use the following thumbnail sketch as a suggested layout for your flyer design.

PLAYER'S NOTES:

CLASS HOUR: ______ DATE: ______ NAME: ______________________

PRACTICE DRILL B-5

Create a Flyer

PRACTICE GOAL TO ACCOMPLISH

As your final drill in this section, you will design a special type of flyer that can be used as the cover on a class report or project. Let the strategies you have learned up to now and your own creativity be your guide for this one.

STRATEGIES TO CONSIDER

Before creating your flyer, note the following suggestions for some basic design hints:

1. Keep in mind that you have only one opportunity to make a first impression with your reader.
2. Be sure the cover includes all the necessary information along with a hint as to what the report contains.
3. Your cover should establish instant appeal and arouse the reader's desire to open the report and see what is inside.
4. You could draw the Greek columns in this report from scratch.

SUPPLIES TO USE

The following information should appear on your flyer design. If you like, use the data and graphic for a different report. You could even make a cover for a report you are currently working on!

TITLE: *A Greek Citadel—Acropolis*

NAME: *Dana Caranci*

CLASS: *World History*

DATE: *October 17, 19—*

GRAPHIC IMAGE: *The Parthenon, a Greek temple, and/or a classic Greek column*

CHART TO FOLLOW

Use the following thumbnail sketch as a suggested layout for your flyer design.

PLAYER'S NOTES:

GUIDELINES FOR SPECIALITY ITEMS

Speciality items are printed materials that are required only by certain businesses or for particular situations rather than items used in general by most businesses. See Figure 3.3. Materials such as menus, tickets, recipe pages, labels, and greeting cards are considered specialty items.

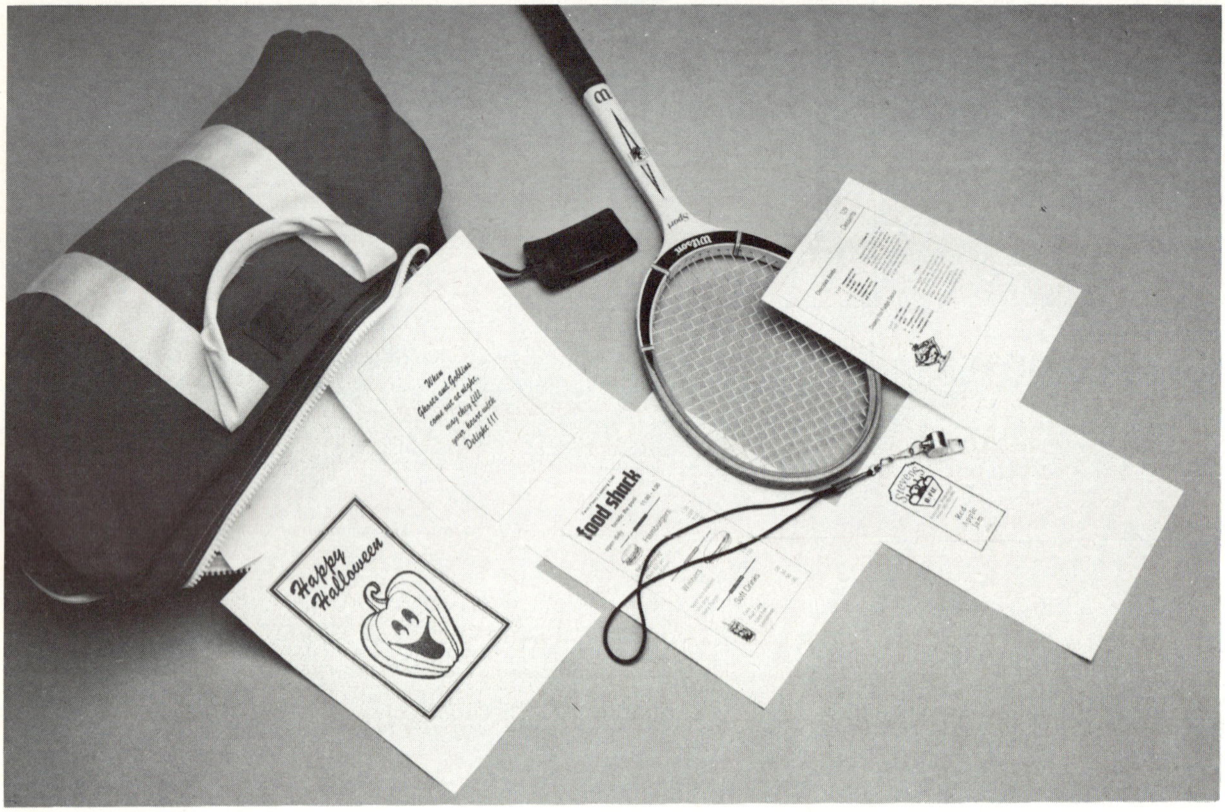

Figure 3.3 You can use desktop publishing to produce a variety of items like menus, tickets, recipe pages, labels, and greeting cards.

POINTS TO CONSIDER

Note the following considerations as you design your speciality items:

1. Often the speciality item is of an unusual size rather than a standard size.
2. The size usually relates to the purpose of the item.
3. Creating and publishing this type of document may be a one-time-only situation for a business. Therefore you may be unable to refer to previous documents for reference.
4. Due to the nature of the item, individual requirements are established by its intended use.
5. Information to be included may be of a specialized nature.

6. This type of document gives an opportunity to be totally creative. Just remember to follow the general design techniques.

7. Many different types of documents may be considered speciality items.

COACH'S CORNER

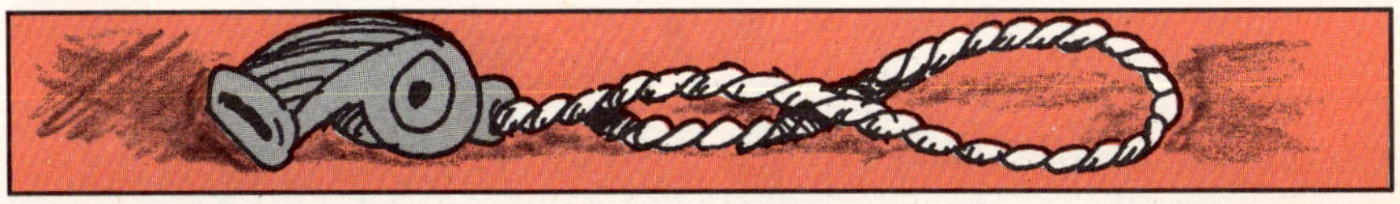

Now it is time to flex your muscles and see what you can do. Your practice up to now has been rather routine. During this session, however, you will work on speciality items that require a different plan of action for each drill. You should enjoy this change of pace. Remember, do not violate any of the strategies as you design these unusual types of documents.

CLASS HOUR: ______ DATE: ______ NAME: ______________________

PRACTICE DRILL C-1

Create a Specialty Item

PRACTICE GOAL TO ACCOMPLISH

The first speciality item you will design is a label that can be used on a product. Other types of labels could be for shipping, a diskette, a visitor's pass, or a name tag, to name just a few examples.

STRATEGIES TO CONSIDER

Before creating your label, note the following suggestions for some basic design hints:

1. Determine an appropriate size and shape for the label according to how and where the label will be attached to the product. Know the size of the product.
2. A graphic image, if appropriate, can communicate the type of product it represents, thus making the product easier to identify.
3. Do not crowd the label with unnecessary information; white space is a design element in itself.
4. For a label to be effective, it must be noticed. Create a design that will catch the viewer's eye.

SUPPLIES TO USE

The following information should appear on your label design. As this is a label for a jar of jam, use an appropriate size for a glass jar. If you like, make a label for a different kind of product.

PRODUCT: *Red Apple Jam*

NAME OF BUSINESS: *Stevens U-Pic*

ADDRESS: *Northport, Washington*

PHONE: *(555) 853-2982*

SIZE: *250 ml*

GRAPHIC IMAGE: *Apples or a basket of apples*

CHART TO FOLLOW

Use the following thumbnail sketch as a suggested layout for your specialty item design.

PLAYER'S NOTES:

CLASS HOUR: ________ DATE: ________ NAME: ____________________

PRACTICE DRILL C-2

Create a Specialty Item

PRACTICE GOAL TO ACCOMPLISH

Now design a ticket for advance sales to a dinner. Other types of tickets could be for a play, musical presentation, car wash, athletic activity, or raffle.

STRATEGIES TO CONSIDER

Before creating your ticket, note the following suggestions for some basic design hints:

1. Think of the ticket you are designing merely as a template. It can be copied several times to fill a standard sheet of paper (8½ by 11 inches) for printing additional tickets.
2. The size and shape of the ticket should be easy for people to handle and read. (COACH'S TIP: Adjust the ticket size to facilitate the placement and cutting of individual tickets on a page.)
3. Contrasting type sizes will aid in the readability of pertinent information contained on the ticket.
4. A graphic image can be included along with the text to add interest. The size should be such that it does not overpower or interfere with the text.

SUPPLIES TO USE

The following information should appear on your ticket design. If you like, use the data and graphic of a different event.

NAME OF EVENT: *57th Family Style Harvest Festival Dinner*

DATE: *Tuesday, October 9, 19--*

TIME: *5:00–7:30 p.m.*

LOCATION: *Arden Grange Hall*

COST: *Adults $6.00, Child (under 10) $3.00*

GRAPHIC IMAGE: *An autumn leaf or other fall symbol*

CHART TO FOLLOW

Use the following thumbnail sketch as a suggested layout for your ticket design.

PLAYER'S NOTES:

CLASS HOUR: ______ **DATE:** ______ **NAME:** ____________________

PRACTICE DRILL C-3

Create a Specialty Item

PRACTICE GOAL TO ACCOMPLISH

This time you will design a greeting card to be used by a business or an individual. Other types of cards could be for notice of relocation, invitation, or announcement.

STRATEGIES TO CONSIDER

Before creating your greeting card, note the following suggestions for some basic design hints:

1. Consider various formats for the card: fold at the top, fold on the left side, fold in quarters, or fold in thirds. (COACH'S TIP: It still may be necessary to cut and paste a final document before printing the actual copies.) You must consider the placement of the cover and the inside message of the card.
2. Coordinate the size and shape of the card with available envelope sizes.
3. For the message, a personal touch can be added by using a script typeface, which imitates handwriting. However, never use all caps in a script font.
4. If you create a card that is to be folded in quarters, consider the fact that the inside message will be in an opposite direction from the cover. You may need to flip the graphic image or inside message to allow for folding the page over.

SUPPLIES TO USE

The following information should appear on your greeting card design. If you like, create a card for a different occasion or holiday.

COVER WORDING: *Happy Halloween*

INSIDE MESSAGE: *When Ghosts and Goblins come out at night, may they fill your heart with Delight!!!*

GRAPHIC IMAGE: *A pumpkin or other appropriate graphic*

CHART TO FOLLOW

Use the following thumbnail sketches as suggested layouts for your greeting card design.

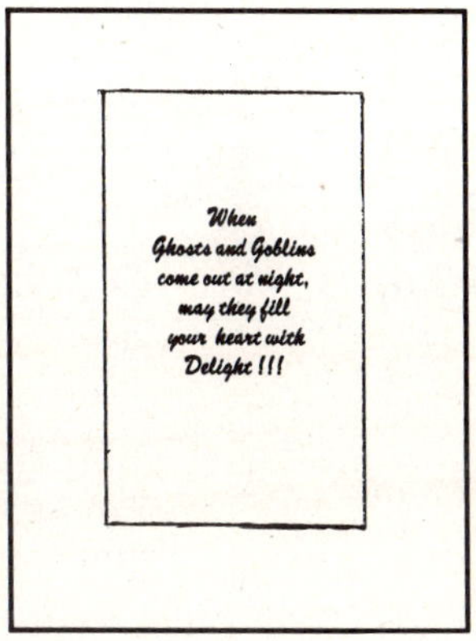

PLAYER'S NOTES:

CLASS HOUR: ______ DATE: ______ NAME: ______________________

PRACTICE DRILL C-4

Create a Specialty Item

PRACTICE GOAL TO ACCOMPLISH

Design a simple menu to be used at a small eating establishment. You can create any kind of menu you want. Other types of menus could be for a catering business, pizza take-out, or even an elaborate menu for a restaurant. You decide on how detailed and elaborate the food selections will be.

STRATEGIES TO CONSIDER

Before creating your menu, note the following suggestions for some basic design hints:

1. A graphic image of an item can create an appeal for that item. However, too many graphics detracts from the listing of the food items.
2. Using a line to separate each section of the menu helps the reader identify the different food sections.
3. Changing typefaces between sections can confuse your reader. If you must change typefaces, have a reason for the change.
4. A column layout is helpful when designing menus—one column for the food item and a second column for the price. It is not necessary for the columns to be the same width. Determine how to create columns with your software.
5. You can use leaders (a row of dots or periods) to connect the food item to the price.

SUPPLIES TO USE

The following information should appear on your menu design. You can use other data to create any kind of menu you want. This information is listed as a suggestion.

NAME OF BUSINESS: *Twin Pines Country Club Food Shack*

LOCATION: *Beside the pool*

HOURS: *Open daily 11:00 to 4:00*

FIRST FOOD ITEMS AND COSTS: *HAMBURGERS: Natural Burger 1.50, Cheeseburger 2.00, Chili Burger 2.00, Olive Burger 2.50*

SECOND FOOD ITEMS AND COSTS: *WEINERS: Beef in a Blanket 1.00, Hot Brat 2.00, Roly Polish 1.50*

DRINKS AND COSTS: *SOFT DRINKS: Cola .50, Diet Cola .50, Iced Tea .50, Lemonade .50*

GRAPHIC IMAGE: *A hamburger, hot dog, drink, or any other appropriate food item*

CHART TO FOLLOW

Use the following thumbnail sketch as a suggested layout for your menu design.

PLAYER'S NOTES:

CLASS HOUR: ______ DATE: ______ NAME: ____________________

PRACTICE DRILL C-5

Create a Specialty Item

PRACTICE GOAL TO ACCOMPLISH

For your last practice drill dealing with speciality items, design one page for a recipe book. You can design a different kind of page, if you like. Other types of pages to design could be for short stories, poems, or songs.

STRATEGIES TO CONSIDER

Before creating your recipe page, note the following suggestions for some basic design hints:

1. Because pages of words tend to be visually uninteresting, provide some illustration to break up the text. Illustrations should present a visual image of the corresponding text.
2. Pages in a book often contain a header, which informs the reader as to the content of the page and/or page number. (COACH'S TIP: Place the header where it is easy to locate. For example, use an outside edge of the page.)
3. Be consistent in how you organize and align the information, or the reader may become confused.
4. When listing items, determine a format that fits the material. Make the list visually easy to read and follow.

SUPPLIES TO USE

The following information should appear on your recipe page design. If you like, you can use any recipe of your choice or design a page of a different type. This information is provided as a suggestion.

HEADER: *Desserts, Page 129*

FIRST RECIPE NAME: *Chocolate Bombe*

FIRST RECIPE INGREDIENTS: *1½ teaspoon gelatine, 1 cup cold water, 1 cup milk, 1½ cups sugar, 2 tablespoons cocoa, 1 teaspoon vanilla, 1 pint heavy cream*

FIRST RECIPE DIRECTIONS: *Yields 1¾ Quarts: Soak gelatine in cold water. Stir and bring to a boiling point the milk, sugar, and cocoa. Dissolve gelatine in the mixture. Cool it. Add the vanilla. Chill the gelatine until it is about to set.*

Whip the heavy cream until stiff; then fold it into the gelatine. Freeze the bombe in a mold or in refrigerator trays.

SECOND RECIPE NAME: *Creamy Hot Fudge Sauce*

SECOND RECIPE INGREDIENTS: *1½ cups sugar, 1½ cups evaporated milk, 2 teaspoons vanilla, 4 oz. unsweetened chocolate, 4 tablespoons butter*

SECOND RECIPE DIRECTIONS: *Yields 2 Cups: Melt together butter and chocolate over very low heat. Slowly add the sugar and milk, stirring until sugar dissolves and mixture starts to thicken. Remove pan from heat and add vanilla. Can be stored in refrigerator for several months. Best to heat sauce slightly before serving.*

GRAPHIC IMAGE: *An ice cream sundae or other appropriate food graphic*

CHART TO FOLLOW

Use the following thumbnail sketch as a suggested layout for your recipe page design.

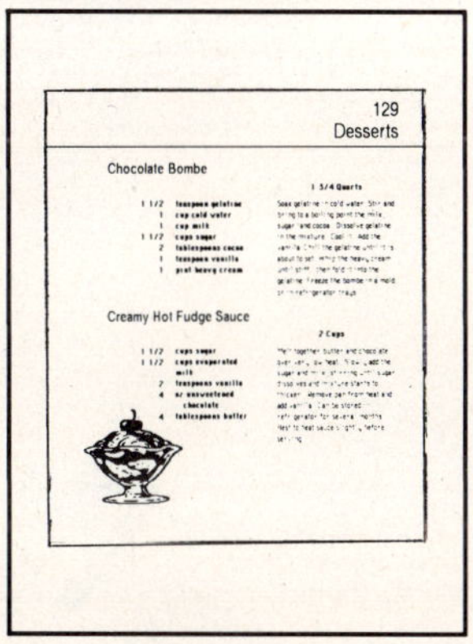

PLAYER'S NOTES:

GUIDELINES FOR BUSINESS FORMS

Business forms are of two types—those used within a company (internal) and those that will leave the company (external). An endless assortment of documents are used to process information while conducting daily business activities. However, the intent of each document is still to effectively communicate information to others. See Figure 3.4. Forms that are used often can be organized in template files. A **template file** stores the master version of the blank form on a data disk. This is then loaded, updated, and saved under a different name on your disk each time a form is to be completed.

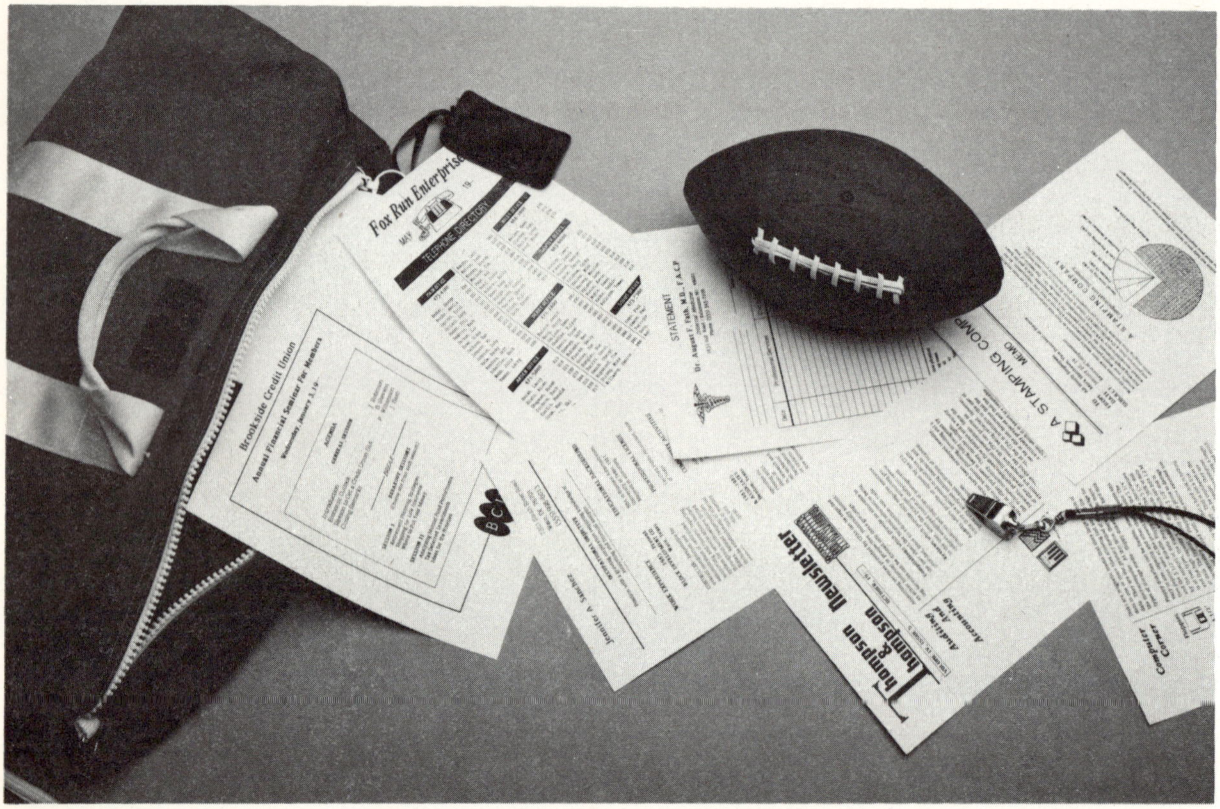

Figure 3.4 Business forms are of two types—those used within a company (internal) and those that will leave the company (external).

POINTS TO CONSIDER

Note the following considerations as you design your business forms:

1. Keep business documents professional in appearance.
2. Develop a company identity by establishing design consistency throughout various company documents.
3. Follow accepted industry size standards where appropriate.
4. Keep future modifications in mind when designing the layout.
5. The design should guide the reader through the document.

6. Establish a series of stored template files for documents that are used repeatedly.
7. Business documents are normally required reading.
8. Provide enough room in each area on the form to accommodate the required data.
9. It is helpful on certain forms to include a form title.
10. Keep a printed file of the documents used in the business for future reference.

COACH'S CORNER

This is your final practice session: the one that decides who earns a position on the starting line-up. To conclude your conditioning, you will "make over" a series of business forms by evaluating the present form and then redesigning it. Your goal is to create a form that more effectively communicates the information. After completing this series of *makeover drills*, you should be in shape to make that *Big Play* during the games ahead.

CLASS HOUR: ______ DATE: ______ NAME: ______________________

PRACTICE DRILL D-1

Create a Business Form

PRACTICE GOAL TO ACCOMPLISH

Redesign an agenda for a company meeting. An **agenda** is a listing of the events that will occur or topics to be discussed in a meeting.

STRATEGIES TO CONSIDER

Before creating your agenda, note the following suggestions for some basic design hints:

1. When the company logo appears on materials, a feeling of instant association and/or recognition is established. (COACH'S TIP: A logo should attract notice without being the dominant element on a business document.)
2. Use various type sizes and type styles to denote the importance of the different activities on the agenda.
3. The total design should remain simple. You can create interest by using box rules to tie together the different parts of the agenda.

SUPPLIES TO USE

A sample of the agenda presently being used appears on the next page. Either use this data for making over the agenda or create a new agenda for a meeting of your choice.

The purpose of this type of document is to provide an outline or listing of the activities taking place at a meeting. This particular meeting is the annual seminar being conducted for members of a credit union.

AGENDA TO MAKE OVER FOR DRILL D-1

BROOKSIDE CREDIT UNION
Annual Financial Seminar for Members
Wednesday, January 3, 19--

A G E N D A
General Session

Introduction . . . . J. Robinson
Economic Outlook . . . . B. Stevens
Reason to Get a Credit Union IRA . . . . P. Williamson
Closing Remarks . . . . J. Baab

* * * * B R E A K * * * *
Breakout Sessions (Choose one from each session)

Session I
* Retirement Planning Stretegies
* Shopping for Life Insurance
* Where to Put Your Money

Session II
* Analyzing Mutual Fund Performance
* Tax Deferred Investments
* Ideas for the Nineties

CHART TO FOLLOW

Use the following thumbnail sketch as a suggested layout for your agenda design. Refer to the agenda above to make over as a comparison.

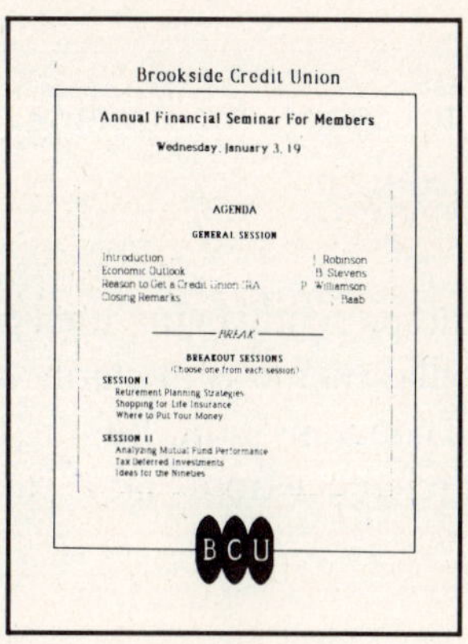

CLASS HOUR: ______ DATE: ______ NAME: ______________________

PRACTICE DRILL D-2

Create a Business Form

PRACTICE GOAL TO ACCOMPLISH

Redesign a company memorandum. The purpose of a **memorandum** is for written communications between personnel within a business.

STRATEGIES TO CONSIDER

Before creating your memorandum, note the following suggestions for some basic design hints:

1. A special heading that includes the company name, logo, and form title can establish a company standard when used consistently on all in-house documents.
2. Using spreadsheet software, try converting the table in the memo to a pie chart. A visual illustration makes the message more interesting and understandable. (COACH'S TIP: If your DTP software will not import charts from a spreadsheet software, print the chart and then cut and paste it on the actual memo. If you do this, don't forget to leave room for the pie chart.)
3. If you cannot add a specific pie chart, improve the appearance of the table.
4. Use ruled lines to separate the heading from the message area.

SUPPLIES TO USE

A sample of the memo presently being used appears on the next page. The content of this particular memo is to clarify any questions employees have concerning their total compensation. Be sure to leave room for the pie chart or table. Change the reference from "table" to "graph" in the third sentence in the memo.

MEMORANDUM TO MAKE OVER FOR DRILL D-2

M E M O R A N D U M

TO: All Hourly Employees
FROM: Mark Matthews, Vice President of Finance
DATE: January 20, 19--
SUBJECT: Review of Compensation

Most employees view their weekly paycheck as their total compensation for services rendered. Actually, your weekly paycheck represents only a fraction of your total compensation. As the following table illustrates, the ''ordinary payroll'' for a typical employee--that is, pay for hours worked--amounted to only 74.4% of total compensation in calendar 19--. The balance of your compensation from A STAMPING COMPANY comes to you in the form of non-cash compensation ranging from holidays (6.2%) to participation in group insurance programs (9.3%).

COMPENSATION SUMMARY

Social Security	1,250	6.1%
Pension	832	4.0%
Health	1,800	8.7%
Life & Disability	114	0.6%
Vacation & Holiday	1,280	6.2%
Ordinary Payroll	15,360	74.4%

We hope that this notice will help you to better understand your compensation. If you have any further questions about your employee benefits, please contact the Personnel Manager.

CHART TO FOLLOW

Use the following thumbnail sketch as a suggested layout for your memorandum design. Refer to the memo to make over above as a comparison.

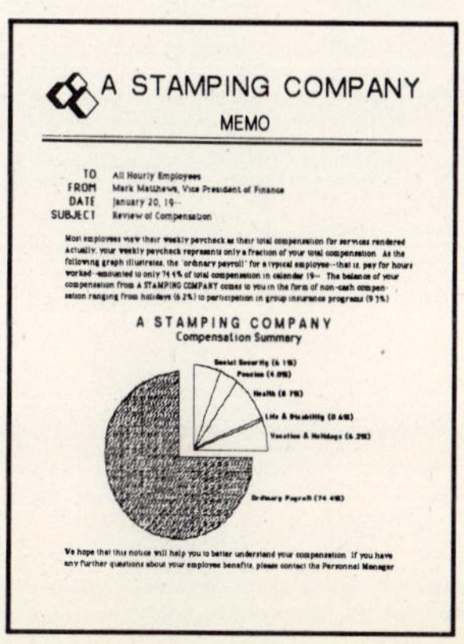

CLASS HOUR: ______ DATE: ______ NAME: ______________________

PRACTICE DRILL D-3

Create a Business Form

PRACTICE GOAL TO ACCOMPLISH

Redesign a page from a company telephone directory. The purpose of a **telephone directory** is to provide a one-page listing of names and phone numbers of company personnel.

STRATEGIES TO CONSIDER

Before creating your telephone directory, note the following suggestions for some basic design hints:

1. Using reversed type for the names of departments, divisions, etc., provides emphasis and divides a long listing into smaller sections.
2. Adjust spacing within the columns so all the columns end at the same point.
3. Numbers should be aligned in each column. (COACH'S TIP: Sometimes numbers are difficult to line up. Using a **monospace typeface**, in which all characters are of the same width, makes this task easier. For example, Courier is a monospace typeface.)
4. Use vertical rules between columns to make the page easier to read.

SUPPLIES TO USE

A sample of the telephone listing presently being used appears on the next page. The document should be easy to identify and information should be arranged in such a way that names and phone numbers can be located quickly.

TELEPHONE DIRECTORY TO MAKE OVER FOR DRILL D-3

F O X R U N E N T E R P R I S E S
TELEPHONE DIRECTORY
May 19--

MAIN OFFICE: 473-4100

Becker, George . . . 224
Bender, Amelia . . . 222
Capizzo, Ferol . . . 251
Gerlach, Gary . . . 219
Hazen, Teri 223
Hembree, Mark . . . 256
Herman, Joe 225
Howe, Diane 254
Jackson, Dan 221
Johnson, Al 252
Johnson, Doty . . . 255
Kelm, Becky 257
Mendoza, Jeff . . . 226
Scheffler, Herb . . 229
Webb, Julie 253
Yonker, Larry . . . 228

ARDEN OFFICE: 471-5000

Borah, Larry 213
Bratu, Allen 218
Chapman, Susan . . . 211
Cordaro, Barb . . . 230
Curtis, Ronald . . . 233
Drum, Ronald 244
Fumiaki, Oki 215
Green, Linda 239
Hiler, Jeanne . . . 217
Limon, Ruben 231
Mandro, Lori 241
Matson, Jack 212
Mooney, Brenda . . . 216
Morlock, Jim 232
Page, Val 218

Rodewald, Jeff . . . 246
Scherer, Holly . . . 214
Sheng, Yang 238
Stolpe, Bill 219
Suwarsky, Debbie . . 234
Torres, Cheryl . . . 242
Ulleg, Bill 243
Zech, Karen 219

DERBY OFFICE: 471-2800

Balsis, David . . . 281
Burg, Jerry 295
Carlson, Dana . . . 293
Chaffee, Eileen . . 286
Davis, Susan 282
Downey, Jeff 281
Eubanks, Bev 291
Flores, Sally . . . 283
Golas, Joe 287
Gungler, Sue 280
Harris, Carol . . . 299
Hauch, Cheryl . . . 284
Hipskind, Tim . . . 292
Strong, Mike 285
Willmeng, Janice . . 288

NILES OFFICE: 468-1000

Aviles, Gwen 272
Cluchey, Judy . . . 271
Harris, Lana 274
Wood, Vicki 273

SAWYER OFFICE: 983-6600

Dunlop, James . . . 202
Fikes, Debra 211
Fulton, George . . . 207
Geik, Jerry 210
Gillham, Corky . . . 219
Gulino, Mike 205
Harvey, Marilyn . . 202
Hyland, Dede 216
Koern, Kevin 212
McKie, James 208
Radke, Debbie . . . 218
Vollrath, Tammy . . 219

SODUS OFFICE: 473-5000

Cayo, Paul 101
Damon, Paula 104
Parrigin, Lucy . . . 105
Soto, Mary 102
Weber, Steve 103

CHART TO FOLLOW

Use the following thumbnail sketch as a suggested layout for your telephone directory design. Refer to the telephone directory to make over on the previous page as a comparison.

PLAYER'S NOTES:

CLASS HOUR: ______ DATE: ______ NAME: ______________________

PRACTICE DRILL D-4

Create a Business Form

PRACTICE GOAL TO ACCOMPLISH

Redesign a professional statement. A **professional statement** is the document used in billing a client for services rendered.

STRATEGIES TO CONSIDER

Before creating your professional statement, note the following suggestions for some basic design hints:

1. Develop a form size that meets your requirements. Usually it is best if a standard size is used, such as 8½ by 11 inches.
2. Make the form easy to understand and complete. The lines should be evenly spaced and provide ample room to fill in the required information.
3. When a business conducts all its activities within its own area code, its phone number may appear without an area code.
4. It is helpful on forms to include a form title.

SUPPLIES TO USE

A sample of the form presently being used appears on the next page. The business is converting to a computer-based billing system. Therefore it is necessary to have this hand-completed form converted into a computer output form.

PROFESSIONAL STATEMENT TO MAKE OVER FOR DRILL D-4

STATEMENT

AUGUST F. FATH, M.D., F.A.C.P.
Internal Medicine
1631 Gull Road
Kalamazoo, MI 49001
(555) 343-7206

DATE	PROFESSIONAL SERVICE	CHARGE		PAID		BALANCE	

CP–Complete physical	UR–Urinalysis	↑
FE–Follow up exam	ML–Multiphase lab. test	PAY LAST
OC–Office call	LAB–Laboratory	AMOUNT
BC–Blood count	INJ–Injections	IN THIS
EKG–Electrocardiogram	C&S–Culture & smear	COLUMN

CHART TO FOLLOW

Use the following thumbnail sketch as a suggested layout for your professional statement design. Refer to the professional statement to make over on the previous page as a comparison.

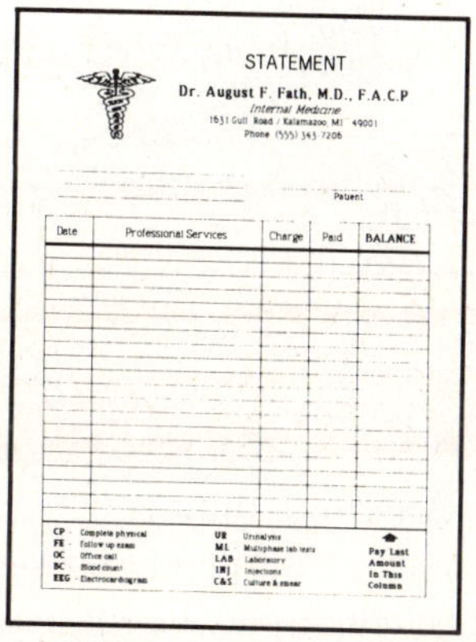

PLAYER'S NOTES:

CLASS HOUR: ______ DATE: ______ NAME: ______________________________

PRACTICE DRILL D-5

Create a Business Form

PRACTICE GOAL TO ACCOMPLISH

Redesign a resume. A **resume** summarizes an individual's professional objectives, work experience, educational background, and other information useful to a prospective employer. A good resume presents a clear image of the person's qualifications.

STRATEGIES TO CONSIDER

Before creating your resume, note the following suggestions for some basic design hints:

1. Arrange and organize each section consistently.
2. Use different type sizes and type styles within the text to clearly identify levels of importance.
3. Shorter lines make the information more readable.
4. Ragged-right margins, present a warmer, friendlier feeling and provide white space in the layout.
5. Overall design should express personality yet maintain a businesslike tone. (COACH'S TIP: This would be an excellent opportunity for you to develop a resume for yourself.)

SUPPLIES TO USE

A sample of the resume presently being used appears on the next page. You can either redesign the resume that is shown here or you can create your own resume. If you create your own resume, make sure that you provide accurate, up-to-date information about your work experience, education, and interests.

RESUME TO MAKE OVER FOR DRILL D-5

JENNIFER A. SANCHEZ
7301 South River Road
Waco, TX 76701
(555) 998-6013

OCCUPATIONAL OBJECTIVE

Position with a growing corporation requiring knowledge of accounting and financial analysis.

WORK EXPERIENCE

1985 - Present	BLOCK DEVELOPMENT CO., Waco, Texas
	CONTROLLER--Responsible for overall coordination and administration of centralized accounting and financial reporting system for several offices located throughout southwestern United States. Related responsibilities include establishment of internal controls, preparation of monthly financial statements, and supervision of payroll.
1981 - 1985	TORRES & ASSOCIATES, Denton, Texas
	ACCOUNTANT--Responsible for planning and supervising audit field work, examination of financial statements, research and application of current technical developments, and formulation of recommendations for systems design with alternative accounting practices.
EDUCATIONAL BACKGROUND	B.B.A. in Business Administration, University of Texas, 1981. Majored in accounting.
PROFESSIONAL LICENSE	Certified Public Accountant, State of Texas
COMMUNITY ACTIVITIES	Acted as Executive Advisor for two years in the Dallas Junior Achievement program, 1984 - 1985. Served as Program Chairperson of the Southwest Economic Club of Waco 1988 - 1990.
PERSONAL	Born November 5, 1959, in Brownsville, Texas. Married with two children. Excellent health.
REFERENCES	Available on request.

CHART TO FOLLOW

Use the following thumbnail sketch as a suggested layout for your resume design. Refer to the resume to make over on the previous page as a comparison.

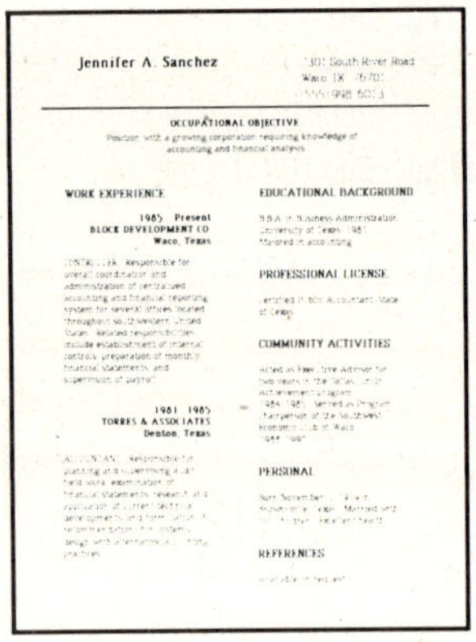
Jennifer A. Sanchez

OCCUPATIONAL OBJECTIVE

Position with a growing corporation requiring knowledge of accounting and financial analysis

WORK EXPERIENCE

1985 Present
BLOCK DEVELOPMENT CO
Waco, Texas

1981 1985
TORRES & ASSOCIATES
Denton, Texas

EDUCATIONAL BACKGROUND

PROFESSIONAL LICENSE

COMMUNITY ACTIVITIES

PERSONAL

REFERENCES

PLAYER'S NOTES:

CLASS HOUR: ______ DATE: ______ NAME: ______________________

PRACTICE DRILL D-6

Create a Business Form

PRACTICE GOAL TO ACCOMPLISH

Redesign a four-page newsletter. Many companies send a **newsletter** to customers on a regular basis to describe services offered, provide up-to-date information on current topics, discuss company viewpoints, and keep in touch with their clientele.

STRATEGIES TO CONSIDER

Before creating your newsletter, note the following suggestions for some basic design hints:

1. The masthead should make a lasting impression by establishing an identity that will make future issues of the newsletter easy to recognize.
2. As a generally accepted practice, headlines (18- to 36-point type) are set in a larger type size than the body copy (10- or 12-point type). However, this is not always true.
3. Headings typed in upper- and lowercase are easier to read than those keyed in all caps.
4. As a method of showing emphasis, use a bold or italic type style sparingly instead of underscoring text. Refrain from putting an entire paragraph in either boldface or italics.
5. The width of your column is determined by the typeface and type size used. (COACH'S TIP: Some common rules say column width should be 9 or 10 words, or 40 to 50 characters per line. However, there is no precise formula.)

SUPPLIES TO USE

A sample of the newsletter presently being used appears on the next four pages. You can update and redesign the newsletter that is provided, or you can create your own newsletter.

NEWSLETTER TO MAKE OVER FOR DRILL D-6

Thompson & Thompson Newsletter

VOLUME IV, ISSUE 5 **OCTOBER 19--**

AUDITING AND ACCOUNTING

Accounting services provided by CPAs can be regarded as either historical or prospective. Historically, accounting services can be divided into three groupings:

> Compilations which provide no assurance to the user about the financial information being provided, since no examination was made.
>
> Reviews which provide only negative assurance to the user, since the principal accounting procedures employed consist of analytical review procedures and inquiries of management.
>
> Audits which provide an opinion by the CPA, since they are performed in accordance with "generally accepted auditing standards" and include independent verification of financial statement balances.

Prospective services have been developed recently, and their value for business planning, investing and a variety of other purposes is being fully recognized by the business community. They include budgets, forecasts, projections, cash flow analysis and a variety of other predictive financial presentations. Since the events are prospective, the CPA can provide no assurance about the results being reflected. However, the involvement of the CPA is invaluable to the user of the data because he or she can determine that the information is accurately prepared and that the assumptions upon which it is based are reasonable.

COMPUTER CORNER

Disks are magnetic media that store large amounts of data in one or more files allowing fast access to the data. They are our primary method of data storage for the microcomputer. At this time, there are two major types of storage media --floppy diskettes and hard disk.

FLOPPIES

Floppy diskettes can be flexible, interchangeable and vary in size, capacity and other characteristics. The two popular sizes at the present time are the 5 1/4" and the 3 1/2" diskette. Floppy disks are characterized by the amount of data they will hold. The 5 1/4" disk is of two types, the standard which holds 360K of data and the high-capacity 5 1/4 " disk which can hold 1.2M of data. The typical capacity for the 3 1/2" disk is approximately 720K. Floppies are prone to damage and must be treated with care to ensure extended use.

HARD DISKS

You have probably heard that a hard disk is nothing more than a "giant" floppy. That is not a true statement. The hard disk can be considered as the control center of your microcomputer. They are usually installed directly into the microcomputer (fixed) or into a protective case, thus assuring a longer life. They also have greater storage capacity and much faster processing speeds than floppies. There are a variety of sizes of hard disks -- for example, 20 Mb, 40 Mb or 80 Mb (Megabytes, millions of characters).

Whether you purchase a microcomputer with a hard disk or plan to upgrade to a hard disk, you should consider the following key features:

Installation type -- internal (installed within the microcomputer system unit) or external (sitting outside the system unit).

Backup Method -- how a duplicate of all or part of the data stored on the hard disk is produced. Backup to floppies takes many diskettes and can be slow unless a special program is purchased; alternative methods are backup to magnetic tape cartridges and hard disk to hard disk.

TAX NOTES

Score one for the IRS! Over the past several years, special agents have been posing as casino patrons and watching cocktail waitresses, bartenders and other personnel at various casinos. They compiled statistics of hourly tips the employees received and extra-polated the data on a yearly basis. Then several IRS audits were undertaken, which showed a very high level of non-compliance in tip reporting, particularly among waitresses. The operation resulted in the assessment of several million dollars in taxes and penalties.

Taxpayers generally dread hearing from the IRS because more often than not, it will be an audit notice. The IRS basically has four levels of dealing with taxpayers when a problem arises. They are:

TYPES OF AUDIT

Correspondence about discrepancies between items on the tax return and the information submitted on information returns filed by banks, brokers and others. These matters can usually be cleared up through the mail.

Service center audits which request the taxpayer to agree to an adjustment of tax by signing a letter of explanation. Such matters may be contested if the taxpayer feels the IRS is wrong.

Office audits which require the taxpayer to make an appointment at the local IRS office and to produce substantiating documentation governing specific areas of the return being scrutinized.

Field audits, in which an IRS agent visits the taxpayer's home or business, by appointment, to audit the return. Field audits usually involve complicated returns or significant areas of audit that will require the review of voluminous data. When criminal wrongdoing is suspected, the field audit may be conducted by a "special" agent. It is essential to obtain legal advice as soon as this becomes known.

PERSONAL FINANCES

RETIREMENT SAVINGS

Your retirement savings will grow much faster if you place your money in a tax-deferred investment. There are many tax-deferred investment alternatives, ranging from individual retirement accounts (IRAs) to annuities. We now have a self-study course available to help you understand the various tax-deferred investment vehicles. This two-hour VHS cassette and a workbook are available for only $99. Call Glenda at (555) 383-7110 to place your order today.

BUY-SELL AGREEMENT

Buy-sell agreements are necesary for the continuity of a closely-held business. There are essentially two types: (1) Cross-purchase agreements, in which the remaining shareholders individually agree to purchase the interest of a deceased, disabled, or departing shareholder, and (2) stock-redemption agreements, in which the corporation redeems the shares. Generally, when there are more than two or three shareholders, the stock redemption agreement is preferred because cross-purchase agreements can become too cumbersome.

THOMPSON & THOMPSON
Certified Public Accountants
4500 Westnedge Avenue
Buckskin, IN 47517

Bulk Rate
U.S. Postage
PAID
Buckskin, IN
Permit No. 23

CHART TO FOLLOW

Use the following thumbnail sketches as suggested layouts for the pages of your newsletter design. Refer to the newsletter to makeover on the previous four pages as a comparison.

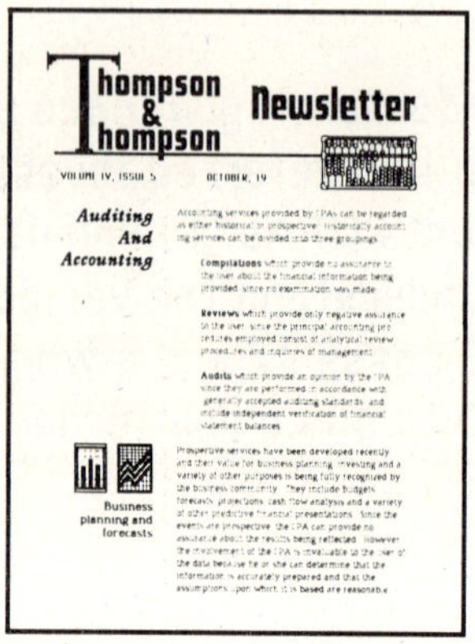
Thompson & Thompson Newsletter

Auditing And Accounting

Business planning and forecasts

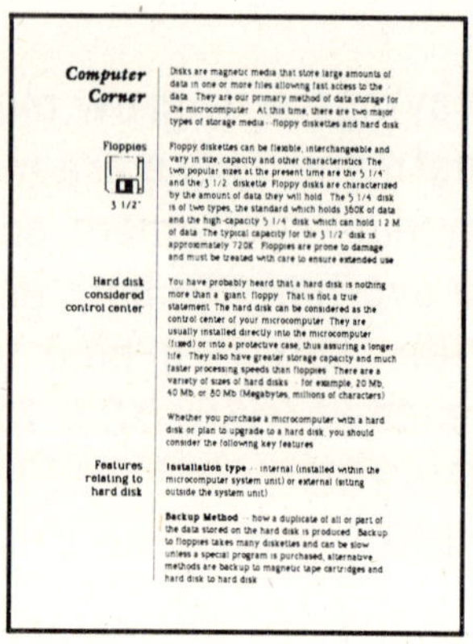
Computer Corner

Floppies

Hard disk considered control center

Features relating to hard disk

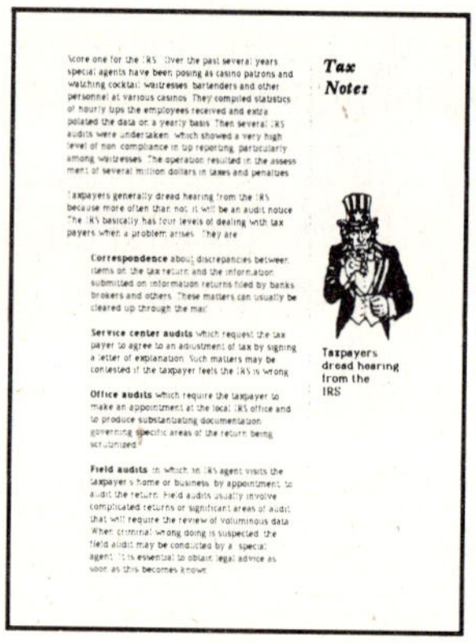
Tax Notes

Taxpayers dread hearing from the IRS

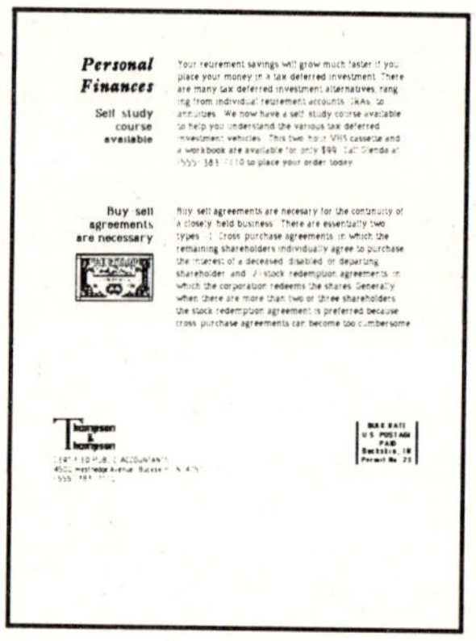
Personal Finances

Self study course available

Buy sell agreements are necessary

PLAYER'S NOTES:

CLASS HOUR: ______ DATE: ______ NAME: ______________________________

THE *Practice Drills* QUIZ

Directions: Complete the following statements and answer the questions.

1. Paper size of ________ by ________ inches is standard for business stationery or flyers.

2. Business documents are normally what type of reading? PLEASURE REQUIRED (Circle the correct answer.)

3. When type has been reversed, it is more difficult to read. TRUE FALSE (Circle the correct answer.)

4. Define a *logo*. ______________________________

____

5. Flyers tend to contain more text than other publications. TRUE FALSE (Circle the correct answer.)

6. Business documents are classified as ______________________, those used within the company, or ______________________, those that leave the company.

7. The maximum number of typefaces to use per page is ______________________.

8. When designing a document, consider your present needs only. TRUE FALSE (Circle the correct answer.)

9. List two factors that should be considered in determining the width of a column.

a. ______________________________

b. ______________________________

10. Which typeface is easiest to read reversed? SERIF SANS SERIF (Circle the correct answer.)

11. List three pieces of information that are included in a letterhead.

a. ______________________________

b. ______________________________

c. ______________________________

12. When you use more than one typeface on a page, it is important that the typefaces complement one another. TRUE FALSE (Circle the correct answer.)

13. The normally accepted type size for headline is ________ to ________ points.

14. A simple design can be effective. TRUE FALSE (Circle the correct answer.)

15. A letterhead height of ________ inches is typical on most stationery.

16. The purpose of a border is to decorate the page. TRUE FALSE (Circle the correct answer.)

17. Explain why a serif typeface is considered a friendlier typeface than sans serif.

____

____

____

18. Identify two ways to achieve contrast or indicate levels of importance in the text when using only one typeface.

a. ______________________________

b. ______________________________

19. Text typed in all capital letters is difficult to read. TRUE FALSE (Circle the correct answer.)

20. The normally accepted type size for body text is ________ to ________ points.

PART 4 The Games

OBJECTIVES

1. To create different DTP documents for a bank in Game 1.
2. To create different DTP documents for a tennis club in Game 2.
3. To create different DTP documents for a travel agency in Game 3.
4. To create different DTP documents for a county fair in Game 4.

INTRODUCTION

Finally, it's the day you have been waiting for—the day of your first *Big Game*! The DTP conditioning is over, and we hope you developed the correct DTP habits and skills. We will soon find out how prepared you are.

According to the schedule, four games are to be played before the *Publishing Season* comes to an end. Each game involves running four plays, which correspond to the four types of drills you worked on while at *practice camp*.

Each play begins with a section identifying the *Play to Execute*, which describes the type of document you are to create. Then, before taking the field, look over the *Tactics to Include*. That section supplies the information you will use in the document. If you have not recorded a winning score after the four plays, you will have a second chance to gain the victory by completing the optional overtime plays. Note that the instructions to the games are very limited. You are expected to know what to do now.

One final reminder from the Coach: successfully playing each game will earn you a DTP varsity letter by the end of the season. Also, there is a chance you will be selected the game's MVP (most valuable player) by scoring the winning designs. Now it is time to take the field; remember, you will call all the signals. Good Luck! And let the games begin!

CLASS HOUR: ______ DATE: ______ NAME: ______________________

GAME 1— PLAY A

Create a Letterhead

PLAY TO EXECUTE

You have been hired to create an appropriate logo for a bank. Then, using this logo, you will design the letterhead stationery and envelope for the bank.

TACTICS TO INCLUDE

1. The following information should appear on the letterhead stationery. For your logo, use a combination of letters, or a symbol that implies *banking*.

NAME OF BANK: *Keystone Country Bank*

ADDRESS: *34 North Garr Road, Dayton, WY 82836*

PHONE: *(555) 377-6000*

GRAPHIC IMAGE: *Design a bank logo.*

2. The following information should appear on the envelope. Indicate a partial or whole envelope border for your printout.

NAME OF BANK: *Keystone Country Bank*

ADDRESS: *34 North Garr Road, Dayton, WY 82836*

GRAPHIC IMAGE: *Use the bank logo you created for the stationery.*

PLAYER'S NOTES:

CLASS HOUR: ________ DATE: ________ NAME: ____________________

GAME 1—PLAY B

Create a Flyer

PLAY TO EXECUTE

Design a flyer that the bank can post in the employees' lounge area announcing the annual golf outing for the year.

TACTICS TO INCLUDE

The following information should appear on the flyer.

EVENT: *10th Annual Bank Golf Outing*

DATE: *Saturday, July 18th*

TIME: *10:00 a.m. Tee-Off*

PLACE: *Green Acres Country Club*

ACTION: *Contact Jeannie For Details*

GRAPHIC IMAGE: *Golf club and ball or other golf image*

PLAYER'S NOTES:

CLASS HOUR: ______ DATE: ________ NAME: ____________________________

GAME 1—PLAY C

Create a Specialty Item

PLAY TO EXECUTE

Design an advertisement that can appear in the local newspaper concerning the bank's certificate of deposit (CD) offerings. The advertisement should be approximately 5⅛ by 7¼ inches in size.

TACTICS TO INCLUDE

The following information should appear in the advertisement. Experiment with the table design. Be sure to use the logo you created in Play A. Add the chart of CD rates in the middle of the page.

NAME OF BANK: *Keystone Country Bank*

HEADING: *CD Rates are going up*

CHART:

TERM	*ANNUAL RATE*	*EFFECTIVE ANNUAL YIELD*
1 year	*8.50%*	*8.83%*
3 year	*8.65%*	*9.00%*
5 year	*8.70%*	*9.05%*

COMMENTS: *Rates offered are subject to change weekly. There is a substantial interest penalty for early withdrawal.*

- *Monthly Compounding*
- *Minimum Deposit $1,000*
- *Deposits Insured to $100,000 by FDIC*

GRAPHIC IMAGE: *Bank logo, hot air balloon, or other appropriate image.*

PLAYER'S NOTES:

CLASS HOUR: ______ DATE: ______ NAME: ______________________

GAME 1—PLAY D

Create a Business Form

PLAY TO EXECUTE

Design a template for bank memorandums. Then, using this form, create a memorandum that contains a stacked bar graph relating to the bank's loan volume.

TACTICS TO INCLUDE

1. The following information should appear on the memorandum template. Store this as a separate file for future reference.

NAME OF BANK: *Keystone Country Bank*

FORM TITLE: *MEMORANDUM*

HEADINGS: *TO:*
FROM:
DATE:
SUBJECT:

GRAPHIC IMAGE: *Use the bank logo.*

2. Using the template that you just created, add the following information in a new file to make a memorandum form about the bank's loan volume.

HEADINGS: *TO: Bank Officers & Supervisors*
FROM: David Ackall, Senior Loan Officer
DATE: January 11, 19—
SUBJECT: Ending Loan Volume

MESSAGE: *The following graph reflects loan volume for the past six years. While growth on mortgages and installment loans has slowed down, management objectives were met through growth in our Commercial Loan Portfolio. An additional factor, not apparent in the graph, is the selling of $3 million in new mortgages in the secondary market.*

GRAPH: Add a stacked bar graph on the bottom of the memo. Use a spreadsheet software to create the graph. Refer to the following table for data. Either cut and paste a printout of the graph, or merge the graph into your DTP software, if possible. Add the last two digits for the four years.

ENDING LOAN BALANCES
(Millions of Dollars)

	19--	*19--*	*19--*	*19--*
MORTGAGE	*21*	*28*	*40*	*30*
COMMERCIAL	*18*	*22*	*23*	*42*
INSTALLMENT	*17*	*20*	*20*	*13*

PLAYER'S NOTES:

CLASS HOUR: ________ DATE: ________ NAME: ______________________________

GAME 1— OVERTIME 1

Create a Brochure

PLAY TO EXECUTE

Design a brochure to place in the bank lobby literature racks explaining a banking service available to the customers. Fold the brochure in half to make a cover, inside two-page spread, and back page. The approximate folded size of the brochure should be 3¼ by 8 inches. In all you will have four pages: cover, two facing inside pages, and the back page.

TACTICS TO INCLUDE

1. The following information should appear on the cover of the brochure. (COACH'S TIP: The cover and back of the brochure would appear on the same page of your design layout.)

BROCHURE TITLE: *The key to your new auto*

GRAPHIC IMAGE: *Car key, bank logo, or any other appropriate image*

2. The following information should appear on the back page of the brochure.

TEXT. *For more information, contact:*
Keystone Country Bank
Loan Department
34 North Garr Road
Dayton, WY 82836
(555) 377-6000

GRAPHIC IMAGE: *Use the bank logo.*

NAME OF BANK: *Keystone Country Bank*

3. The following information should appear on the inside two-page spread of the brochure.

TITLE AT TOP OF TWO PAGES: *A Keystone Country Bank loan can be the key to the car you've always wanted. . .and lots more!*

TEXT WITH HEADINGS: *At Keystone Country Bank, automobiles that are less than five model years old and are used for personal rather than business purposes may serve as collateral for automobile loans. For purposes of determining the age of an automobile, model years change on September 30 of each year for used vehicles and on December 31 each year for new vehicles. Trucks with* *a payload capacity of less than two tons and a passenger capacity of 12 persons or less are included within the definition of "automobiles" under this program.*

Loan Amounts and Interest Rates

Automobile loans may be obtained in any amount from $500 to $20,000. Interest rates will vary from time to time based on the age of the automobile, the amount of your down payment, and general economic conditions.

Loan Terms and Monthly Payments

The minimum term for all automobile loans is six months. The maximum loan term can be as long as five years depending on the age of the vehicle, the amount of the loan, and general economic conditions. The monthly payment for all automobile loans is calculated so that the loan will be fully paid at the end of its term.

Basic Automobile Loan Requirements

The automobile offered as collateral must be adequate security for the loan. Typically, we will determine the loan value for a particular automobile from publication guides in standard use in the automobile financial industry. In some cases it may be necessary to conduct an appraisal of the automobile.

Applying for an Automobile Loan

At Keystone Country Bank, you have the right to file a written automobile loan application on our forms. To assure that we have all the facts needed for consideration of your application, verbal applications are not accepted.

Simple Interest Feature Can Save You Money

At Keystone Country Bank, interest on your automobile loan is changed only on the unpaid balance. With a simple interest automobile loan, you will actually save money on interest charges when you make additional payments or repay your loan early. There is no prepayment change or early payment penalty.

PLAYER'S NOTES:

CLASS HOUR: ______ DATE: ______ NAME: ______________________

GAME 1— OVERTIME 2

Create a Job Description Form

PLAY TO EXECUTE

Design a job description form for the personnel department. The form will be used to develop a booklet containing relevant information on all positions within the bank.

TACTICS TO INCLUDE

The following information should appear on the job description form.

JOB TITLE: *Position: TELLER*

TEXT WITH HEADINGS: *Reports To: Branch Manager/Head Teller*
Job Scope: Serves the public by accepting currency, coins, checks, receipts, or withdrawal slips and processing these items as directed; manages a fund of cash.

RESPONSIBILITIES:

1. *Serves customers at a window processing a variety of transactions using own judgment within narrow limits regarding the validity of transactions presented. Refers questionable transactions to the Head Teller/Branch Manager.*
2. *Receives commercial and individual checking deposits, land contract payments, verifies cash and endorsements, and issues receipts.*
3. *Accepts checks for cashing or paying; verifies endorsements, validity and funds, makes change.*
4. *Sells money orders, cashier's checks, U.S. Savings bonds, and Traveler's checks.*
5. *Functions as the bank's primary contact with the public.*
6. *Required to meet "Standards of Performance" for Teller.*
7. *Other duties as assigned by Supervisor.*

REQUIREMENTS:

1. *High School Graduate.*
2. *Knowledge of how to use an adding machine, typewriter, and check encoder.*
3. *Ability to deal tactfully and efficiently with the public.*
4. *Ability to handle confidentiality.*

GRAPHIC IMAGE: *Use the bank logo.*

COACH'S CORNER

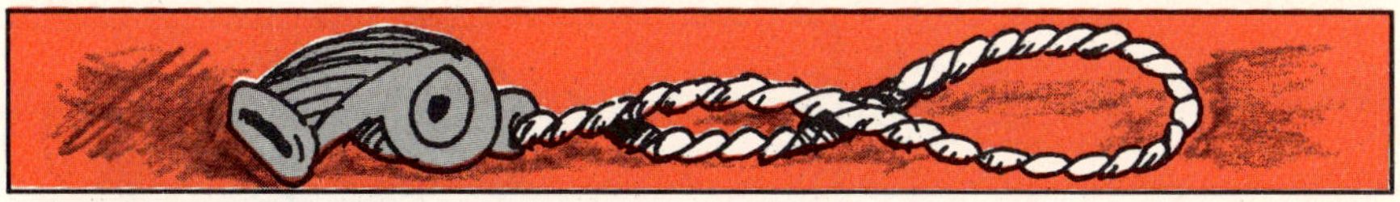

The Coach congratulates the team on their first victory of the season. Great game! The extra effort you put forth during the practice drills to learn different strategies and techniques gave you the edge needed to be the winner in the game with the *Keystone Country Bank.* Remember: As you read and react to each situation, you should follow your game plan; use basic strategies, play within your strengths, and try not to get too fancy in completing the plays.

If injuries occurred, let's hope they were only minor bruises and you are anxious for Game 2 to start. The opposition will line up a little differently in the second game, so make the necessary adjustments.

PLAYER'S NOTES:

CLASS HOUR: ______ DATE: ______ NAME: ______________________

GAME 2— PLAY A

Create a Letterhead

PLAY TO EXECUTE

Create an appropriate logo for a tennis club. Then, using this logo, design the letterhead stationery for the club and a notepad for one of the club professionals.

TACTICS TO INCLUDE

1. The following information should appear on the letterhead stationery.

NAME OF CLUB: *the TENNIS CLUB*

ADDRESS: *3200 Tennis Court, Grand Haven, MI 49417*

PHONE: *282-1800 (optional)*

GRAPHIC IMAGE: *Design a club logo. Use a suitable tennis theme.*

2. The following information should appear on the notepad. This will have a smaller trim size than the stationery. You decide on the dimensions of the notepad.

NAME OF CLUB: *the TENNIS CLUB*

PROFESSIONAL: *Bev Linn, Club Pro.*

GRAPHIC IMAGE: *Use the same club logo you designed for the stationery.*

PLAYER'S NOTES:

CLASS HOUR: ______ DATE: ______ NAME: ______________________

GAME 2— PLAY B

Create a Flyer

PLAY TO EXECUTE

Design a flyer to post on the bulletin boards at the tennis club to announce current tennis lesson rates.

TACTICS TO INCLUDE

The following information should appear on the flyer. Add the table of lesson rates at the bottom of the page.

NAME OF CLUB: *the TENNIS CLUB*

HEADLINE: *LESSONS*

FACTS ABOUT LESSONS: *Members and non-members may take lessons from club professional teaching staff. Private, semi-private, or group lessons may be arranged by contacting desk staff personnel.*

PROFESSIONAL STAFF: *Head Professional, Bob Koch; Club Professionals, Beverly Linn, Sally Lopez, Bill Rahn*

LESSON RATES TABLE:

LESSON RATES	*MEMBER*	*NON-MEMBER*
private	*$27.00*	*$30.00*
semi-private	*$14.50*	*$15.00*
3 students	*$10.00*	*$11.00*
4 students	*$9.00*	*$10.00*
5 students	*$8.00*	*$9.00*
6 and over	*$7.00*	*$8.00*

GRAPHIC IMAGE: *Use the club logo, tennis racquet, or other tennis image.*

PLAYER'S NOTES:

CLASS HOUR: ______ DATE: ________ NAME: ______________________________

GAME 2—PLAY C

Create a Specialty Item

PLAY TO EXECUTE

Design a gift certificate that the tennis club can sell during its campaign for club membership. You decide on the dimensions of the certificate. Remember that you need to design both the front and back of the gift certificate. The certificate can also be designed as a folded card (one sheet of paper, folded over once), with the design on the cover and message on the inside.

TACTICS TO INCLUDE

The following information should appear on the gift certificate. You decide what goes on the front and back of the certificate. In the message area, include two blank lines to write names for "TO" and "FROM."

NAME OF CLUB: *the TENNIS CLUB*

ADDRESS: *3200 Tennis Court, Grand Haven, Michigan*

TITLE: *GIFT CERTIFICATE for "Health Fitness and Fun"*

MESSAGE: *Upon presentation of this GIFT CERTIFICATE for "Health Fitness and Fun" bearer is entitled to $75.00 off Membership initiation and one "Free" day.*

TO: ______________________________

FROM: ______________________________

Expires 10/31/—
Not valid with any other membership offerings

GRAPHIC IMAGE: *Use the club logo or other tennis image.*

PLAYER'S NOTES:

CLASS HOUR: ______ DATE: ______ NAME: ______________________

GAME 2— PLAY D

Create a Business Form

PLAY TO EXECUTE

Design a membership application form that can be used by the tennis club for prospective members to fill out when applying for membership to the club.

TACTICS TO INCLUDE

1. The following heading should appear on the application form.

NAME OF CLUB: *the TENNIS CLUB*

ADDRESS: *3200 Tennis Court, Grand Haven, MI 49417*

FORM TITLE: *Membership Application*

GRAPHIC IMAGE: *Use the club logo or other tennis image.*

2. Use lines and/or boxes for the applicant to fill in to complete the form. These should provide the following pieces of information. You could use a checklist for the types of membership.

- *Complete Name (Last Name, First Name, Initial)*
- *Street, City, State, ZIP Code*
- *Telephone Number (Home, Business)*
- *Spouse's Name*
- *Children's Names and Ages*
- *Type of Membership (Single, Family, Couple, Junior)*
- *Date*
- *Signature*

3. A separate section should be added for the tennis club office to complete. Set this off in a box rule at the bottom of the form. Use the following pieces of information.

For Office Use Only

Amount: $__________

Check: #__________

Date: ____/____/____

Rec'd By: __________

CLASS HOUR: ______ DATE: ______ NAME: ____________________

GAME 2— OVERTIME 1

Create a Calendar

PLAY TO EXECUTE

Design a calendar that lists the activities happening at the tennis club for the month. You might save the design as a template before entering information so you have the blank form ready for each month.

TACTICS TO INCLUDE

The following information should appear on the calendar. Draw a seven-day grid and label each day with the appropriate activities. May 1 is a Friday. Add a special section at the bottom of the calendar where special appointments to remember can be written. Use several blank rules.

NAME OF CLUB: *the TENNIS CLUB*

MONTH: *May*

DAILY ACTIVITIES:

May 1, Mixed Doubles Drop Ins, 7:00 pm
2, Men's Day, 11:00 am
3, Mixed Doubles Round Robin, 2:00 pm
5, Ladies' Day, 11:00 am
7, Ladies' Round Robin, 11:00 am
9, Men's Day, 11:00 am
11, Mixed Drop Ins, 11:00 am
12, Ladies' Day, 11:00 am
14, Ladies' Round Robin, 11:00 am
15, Mixed Doubles Drop Ins, 7:00 pm
16, Men's Day 11:00 am
17, Mixed Doubles Round Robin, 2:00 pm
19, Ladies' Day, 11:00 am
20, Men's Round Robin, 7:00 pm
21, Ladies' Round Robin, 11:00 am
23, Men's Day, 11:00 am
24, OPEN HOUSE
25, Mixed Drop Ins, 11:00 am
26, Ladies' Day, 11:00 am
28, Ladies' Round Robin, 11:00 am
30, Men's Day, 11:00 am

SECTION AT BOTTOM HEADING: *APPOINTMENTS TO REMEMBER:*

GRAPHIC IMAGE: *Use the club logo and other appropriate images.*

CLASS HOUR: ______ DATE: ______ NAME: ______________________

GAME 2— OVERTIME 2

Make Over a Newsletter

PLAY TO EXECUTE

Redesign the tennis club's newsletter.

TACTICS TO INCLUDE

A sample of the present newsletter appears on the next two pages. The newsletter is sent to all club members on a quarterly basis to inform them of activities happening at the club.

As you make over the newsletter, it is not necessary to use an 8½ by 11 inch page. You may want to try a different size. What about designing an entirely new masthead, which may or may not include the club logo? And don't forget the possibility of using appropriate graphic images as you arrange the articles in the order that you desire. Doing a makeover allows for experimenting and trying many different ideas.

NEWSLETTER TO MAKE OVER FOR GAME 2—OVERTIME 2—PAGE 1

the TENNIS CLUB
3200 Tennis Court
Grand Haven, MI 49417

"THE RACQUET"

SPRING NEWSLETTER

Members and Friends,

Spring is here and before long, summer will be upon us. Your club, the TENNIS CLUB, like the seasons, has taken a new direction toward promoting health and fitness through racquet sports. With the addition of our Fitness/Nautilus Center, we now can better utilize space and reduce overhead costs. We will be providing fitness programs for the current members along with attracting new members to our Fitness/Nautilus Center.

Tennis and racquetball will continue to be our #1 priority as we keep abreast with industry trends and achieve business goals to provide the best facilities, staffing and programs you would expect from a full service club. As the seasons change, so is your club in hopes of meeting your needs.

Sven Erickson, General Manager

* *

WELCOME OUR NEW MEMBERS!!!

Lloyd Wetzel *** Sue Anne Alvarez *** Will Koch *** Hazel Hass *** Chien Wang *** Don Kretchman *** Kevin Bartz *** Gil & Linda Hasso *** Patti Faraone *** Scott McMillen *** Jennifer Smith *** Bill Gifford *** Gerald Barefield *** Ron Curtis *** Yoko Mitsui *** Benji Dazai *** Patti Wood *** Barb Wicker *** Gary Caranci *** Carl & Sue Olson *** Damian Gonzalez *** Tom Perez *** Jim & Sally Behlen *** Karen Faulkner *** Nanci Capizzo *** Olive Kiger *** Harvey Johnson *** Hortencia Sanchez *** Joe Geary *** Chris Brohman *** Art Weaver *** Deb Schneider *** John Moore *** Kay Stover *** Sonya Reitz *** Lori Shembarger *** Nicol Whitney *** Terri Getz *** Carmen & Bertha Leal

* *

CLAY COURT

For the summer we are offering a "Clay Court Pass" which entitles you to UNLIMITED play on our six outdoor, clay courts for the entire summer.
EACH PASS: $50.00
SPECIAL BONUS: Clay Court Pass will be good for travel team practices, Special Activities (such as Tuesday Night Men's League, etc.) as well as random bookings! ALSO, includes a lesson with Bob on a soft clay court.

UPCOMING EVENTS

- April 6 - Junior Development
- April 10 - High School Tennis Invitational
- April 18 - Fitness Evaluation
- April 20 - USTA/WTA Junior Free Day Clinic
- April 23 - League "Play Off"
- April 25 - Member/Guest Tournament
- April 27 - Spring Leagues Begin
- April 30 - Ladies Tournament

NEWSLETTER TO MAKE OVER FOR GAME 2—OVERTIME 2—PAGE 2

J U N I O R   D E V E L O P M E N T

the TENNIS CLUB offers instructional clinics for Juniors of all age levels, from beginners to tournament players, thus allowing continuing advancement within the club under the capable and experienced guidance of our tennis professionals. All clinics run 2 hours with a maximum of 24 students per session. To register pick up a form at the front desk and return it to the club as soon as possible. Sign-up is on a "first come, first serve" basis.

FEATURES

Player Report--A progress report will be mailed to the home at the completion of the session. Sibling Discount--A 10% discount will be applied to the second child's fees when more than one child per family participates. Walk-on Court Time Discount--All Junior Development participants receive half price "walk-on" court time. Organized Junior Leagues--All players can participate in the Junior League Competition. Prizes will be awarded on the last day of play.

LEVELS OF PLAY

Munchkin Tennis--For those who are just beginning our wonderful game, emphasis is on fun while learning sound fundamentals to build on in the following years.
Level I--For those Juniors, ages 9-14, who have little playing experience. These Juniors will be introduced to the accepted grip, stance, and execution of techniques along with tennis etiquette and rules of the game.
Level II--This group is geared to the player who can rally and has some exposure to the game. Our intent is to make the players into committed players with sound techniques.
Competitive--Designed for the Junior who can play and enjoys competition. We will strive to instill sound stroke production, competitive tactics, and a positive mental attitude.

* *

J O I N   T H E   C L U B

"Join the Club" program now thru May 3rd...we are asking you to be a part of our "Join the Club" promotion during the month of April. Here is how it works: New members joining, pay full initiation fee but won't have to pay any monthly dues until September 1st. To get them started, we will even throw in a one hour tanning session; fitness appraisal and program and/or one hour private racquetball or tennis lesson.

Help us reach our goal of 50 new memberships. By sponsoring a new member, you will receive a club T-shirt. Get a guest pass at the front desk and bring a prospective member to the club and you will be entered in our CLUB AMBASSADOR DRAWING. Win your own private parking spot, tanning sessions, use of locker, private lesson and more! The drawing will be held on Friday, May 1st during our Pasta Party at the club.

PLAYER'S NOTES:

COACH'S CORNER

How about *the TENNIS CLUB*—did they make you struggle to win? And what about the newsletter makeover during the second overtime play? Was it a snap? The going can get tough when you must complete the plays all on your own.

It looks like you are developing a series of play patterns that will be helpful to you in the remaining games. The word is that the competition ahead will be a challenge. So be patient, play smart, and wait for the right opportunity to blitz. You might find it helpful to review strategies prior to starting the game with *Cruises & Tours International*.

CLASS HOUR: ______ DATE: ______ NAME: ____________________

GAME 3— PLAY A

Create a Letterhead

PLAY TO EXECUTE

Create an appropriate logo for a travel agency. Then, using this logo, design the agency's letterhead stationery and a business card for one of the travel agents.

TACTICS TO INCLUDE

1. The following information should appear on the letterhead stationery.

NAME OF AGENCY: *Cruises & Tours International*

ADDRESS: *2606 Lakeshore Drive, Detroit, MI 48200*

PHONE: *(555) 983-7447*

GRAPHIC IMAGE: *Design an appropriate travel agency logo.*

2. The following information should appear on the business card. You decide on the the card's dimensions.

NAME OF AGENCY: *Cruises & Tours International*

ADDRESS: *2606 Lakeshore Drive, Detroit, MI 48200*

PHONE: *(555) 983-7447*

TRAVEL AGENT: *Lowell Vitangcol*

GRAPHIC IMAGE: *Use the logo you designed for the stationery.*

PLAYER'S NOTES:

CLASS HOUR: ______ DATE: ______ NAME: ______________________

GAME 3— PLAY B

Create a Flyer

PLAY TO EXECUTE

Design a flyer that the travel agency can use to announce and promote a special upcoming cruise they are sponsoring.

TACTICS TO INCLUDE

The following information should appear on the flyer.

HEADING: *Caribbean Cruise*

DATE OF CRUISE: *March 5–12*

FACTS ABOUT CRUISE: *Fly free round trip to sunny Florida and sail on to tropical Playa Del Carmen and Cozumel, Mexico, exotic Jamaica and beachy Grand Cayman Island!!!!!*
Deposit of $200 per person is needed to reserve space.

PHONE: *For More Details Call 983-7447*

NAME OF AGENCY: *Cruises & Tours International*

GRAPHIC IMAGE: *Palm tree, palm branches with dancer, or other tropical image.*

PLAYER'S NOTES:

CLASS HOUR: ______ DATE: ______ NAME: ______________________________

GAME 3— PLAY C

Create a Specialty Item

PLAY TO EXECUTE

Design a luggage tag that the travel agency can use as a promotional item. The travel agent will give the luggage tags to clients who book their travel arrangements through the agency. You decide on the dimensions of the luggage tag. As you draw the border, you can indicate how the tag is fastened to the luggage. If you are really adventuresome, draw the entire tag with the chain/strap to attach.

TACTICS TO INCLUDE

1. You need to design the front and back of the tag. The following information should appear on the front side of the luggage tag.

NAME OF AGENCY: *Cruises & Tours International*

ADDRESS: *2606 Lakeshore Dr., Detroit, MI 48200*

PHONE: *(555) 983-7447*

GRAPHIC IMAGE: *Use the travel agency logo.*

2. The following information should appear on the back side of the luggage tag. The owner of the luggage can then fill in the information on the blank lines.

NAME: ______________________

STREET: ______________________

CITY/STATE: ______________________

PHONE: ______________________

PLAYER'S NOTES:

CLASS HOUR: ______ DATE: ________ NAME: ______________________

GAME 3— PLAY D

Create a Newsletter

PLAY TO EXECUTE

Design for the travel agency a newsletter containing information about upcoming cruises, tours, vacation packages, and other items of interest for travelers. The newsletter will be sent to clients and made available in the agency office.

TACTICS TO INCLUDE

1. The following information should appear in the masthead of the newsletter.

MASTHEAD: *Cruise News, Cruises & Tours International, Call 983-SHIP (7447)*

GRAPHIC IMAGE: *Use the travel agency logo.*

2. The following information should be used for a feature article on the front page of the newsletter. Indent the table of times as shown.

Come to Our Second Annual Caribbean Cruise & Tour Show
Welcome Aboard ! ! !
October 7, 19-- from 7:00 p.m. - 9:30 p.m.

The French Chef Restaurant - Crossroads

7:00 - 8:00	*Opening Ceremonies - Door Prizes* *Meet the Sales Reps. - Cash Bar*
8:00 - 8:30	*Introduction of Staff from Cruises and Tours* *Short talk on "Evening Specials"*
8:30	*Buffet Opens - "Carved Steamboat Round of Beef"* *with rolls, fruit and hors d' oeuvres. Cash Bar*
9:00 - 9:30	*A unique show of fashions from "around town" performed by our own Cruises & Tours International Staff with live music! ! !*
9:30	*Grand Prize Drawing! ! ! Free Cruise! ! ! Free airline tickets! ! !*

$4.00 ADVANCE TICKETS (Two chances for the grand prize, a complimentary glass of wine at The French Chef)
$5.00 AT THE DOOR (One chance to win the grand prize)

You will have an opportunity to meet with representatives of the major cruise ships and luxury ocean liners along with the airlines.

---

3. The following items should appear on the second page of the newsletter.

HEADER: *Cruise News, Page 2*

HEADLINE: *Pack your bags and join us for one of our Special Spring Cruises.*

4. The following information should be used for remaining articles in the newsletter. The articles are numbered, but you can arrange them in any order you desire. Use a variety of graphic designs where appropriate. Use vertical rules.

ARTICLE HEADING AND TEXT: *#1—February 15–21*
Sail on a 7 night cruise of a lifetime. Fly free round trip to sunny Florida and take off to the exciting Caribbean! Visit tropical Playa Del Carmen and Cozumel, Mexico, exotic Jamaica! $869.00 per person. Get your ticket to paradise!

ARTICLE HEADING AND TEXT: *#2—March 5–11*
Take a 7 night cruise for a sun drenched vacation to the Carribbean. They have many exciting ports of call including St. Thomas, St. Maarten, San Juan, Barbados, and Martinique. Fly round trip from Chicago to San Juan. Prices start at $1163 per person/double occupancy. Some of life's greatest adventures await!!!

ARTICLE HEADING AND TEXT: *#3—April 10–24*
Cruise through the wonders of the Eastern Caribbean. Visit the most talked about ports of call—San Juan, St. Thomas, Nassau, and the capital of the British Virgin Islands, Tortola. Take the deal of the century to fun in the sun!! Starting at only $1224 for an outside cabin. Book your cruise today.

ARTICLE HEADING AND TEXT: *Staff Meanderings*
LIBBY - Recently, I had the opportunity to cruise transatlantic from Southampton, England to New York City on the newly refurbished QE2. She is truly the "Grande Dame" of the seas. The dining room I was seated in (there are four dining rooms) was called the "Queen's Grill". It is rated in the top 10 of restaurants in England! The food was spectacular! The ship was beautiful. Try it!

SANDY - I have just returned from Spain, where I was able to visit Madrid, Toledo, Malaga and Granada. The history is overwhelming as you walk through a castle where Christopher Columbus also walked. I dined in the world's oldest restaurant, which was Hemingway's favorite! If history doesn't interest you, there's always the lovely beaches of the Costa Del Sol area. Or depending on the season, the snow skiing is great!

PLAYER'S NOTES:

CLASS HOUR: ______ DATE: ______ NAME: ______________________

GAME 3— OVERTIME 1

Create an Advertisement

PLAY TO EXECUTE

Design an advertisement for the travel agency to use in the yellow pages of the telephone directory. The advertisement size should be approximately 6¼ by 2½ inches.

TACTICS TO INCLUDE

The following information should appear in the advertisement. List the services in two columns to save space.

NAME OF AGENCY: *Cruises & Tours International*

ADDRESS: *2606 Lakeshore Drive, Detroit*

PHONE: *983-7447*

HOURS: *Mon–Fri 8:30 am–5:30 pm*

OWNERS: *Eddie Olin, CTC and Libby Cooney*

SERVICES: *Airline Tickets, Cruises, Tour Packages, Rail/Car, Domestic & International Tours, Charters, Group Tours, Hotel Packages, Free Video Library*

GRAPHIC IMAGE: *Use the travel agency logo.*

PLAYER'S NOTES:

CLASS HOUR: ______ DATE: ______ NAME: ____________________

GAME 3— OVERTIME 2

Create an Announcement Card

PLAY TO EXECUTE

Design a card that the travel agency can send to its clients introducing a travel agent who has just joined their agency. You must design both the front and back of the card. You decide on its dimensions.

The announcement can also be designed as a folded card (one sheet of paper, folded over once), with the design on the cover and message on the inside.

TACTICS TO INCLUDE

The following information should appear on the card. On the front of the card, use the name, address, and phone of the agency. On the back of the card, include the message.

NAME OF AGENCY: *Cruises & Tours International*

ADDRESS: *2606 Lakeshore Drive, Detroit, MI 48200*

PHONE: *(555) 983-7447*

MESSAGE: *MAKING WAVES ! ! ! !*
We are proud to announce that
ROSALIE CAPIZZO
has come aboard
Cruises & Tours International
Call ROE
983-7447
to make your travel arrangements

GRAPHIC IMAGE: *Use the travel agency logo.*

PLAYER'S NOTES:

COACH'S CORNER

Now that the season is under way and you have a winning streak going, what do you think? Is playing in a game situation, where it is up to you to actually run the offense, different from a guided practice session? Did the practice drills provide enough training to prepare you sufficiently for playing the games?

Up to now you have been calling each play and executing it with precision to capture the win. However, do not become overconfident! We will see how you manage as the pressure builds in the final game of the season. Can you keep a perfect record and win the championship? Remember, the *Spring Harbor County Fair* will be out to break your winning streak. So, play it safe as you Go For It! Remember, you may have to change your strategy at the line of scrimmage when you see how the defense lines up. Good Luck!

CLASS HOUR: ______ DATE: ______ NAME: ______________________

GAME 4—PLAY A

Create a Letterhead

PLAY TO EXECUTE

Create an appropriate logo for a county fair. Then use this logo to design the fair's letterhead stationery. For this logo, consider all the symbols that make up a county fair—agriculture, animals, farming, cooking, sewing, rides, games, foods, etc.

TACTICS TO INCLUDE

The following information should appear on the letterhead stationery.

NAME OF FAIR: *Spring Harbor County Fair*

ADDRESS: *9122 Center Road, Green Mountain, IA 50637*

PHONE: *(555) 471-3011*

GRAPHIC IMAGE: *Design an appropriate county fair logo.*

PLAYER'S NOTES:

CLASS HOUR: ______ DATE: ______ NAME: ____________________

GAME 4—PLAY B

Create a Flyer

PLAY TO EXECUTE

Design a flyer announcing the tractor pull contest that will be held at the county fair.

TACTICS TO INCLUDE

The following information should appear on the flyer.

NAME OF EVENT: *Tractor Pull Contest*

LOCATION: *Spring Harbor County Fair*

PRIZE: *$1500 Grand Prize*

DATE: *Monday, August 13, 19—*

TIME: *6:30 p.m.*

COST: *Entry Fee $25*

GRAPHIC IMAGE: *Show a person on tractor or other farming-related image and use the fair logo.*

PLAYER'S NOTES:

CLASS HOUR: ______ DATE: ______ NAME: ____________

GAME 4—PLAY C

Create a Specialty Item

PLAY TO EXECUTE

Design a certificate to give to the grand champion winner in each division of the animal entries. Plan the certificate so it will be easy to change the kind of animal and its picture for each category. Use an appropriate certificate border.

TACTICS TO INCLUDE

The following information should appear on the award certificate. Add blank lines for the peoples names.

NAME OF FAIR: *Spring Harbor County Fair*

YEAR: *19—*

MESSAGE: *Grand Champion Lamb awarded to:*

LINES TO WRITE: *Winner's Name, Fair President's Name*

GRAPHIC IMAGE: *Use a lamb or other animal, and a fancy border around the certificate*

PLAYER'S NOTES:

CLASS HOUR: ________ DATE: ________ NAME: ______________________________

GAME 4—PLAY D

Create a Business Form

PLAY TO EXECUTE

Design a form that can be used by the judges as they evaluate the exhibits. The form will be used to record information pertaining to the specific class and the judge's evaluation of the individual exhibits.

TACTICS TO INCLUDE

1. The following heading should appear on the judge's form.

NAME OF FAIR: *Spring Harbor County Fair*

FORM TITLE: *JUDGE'S WORKSHEET*

GRAPHIC IMAGE: *Use the fair logo.*

2. Provide blank lines for the judge to enter as form headings for the following items. Put these at the top of the form.

- *Page No., Date, Clerk*

3. Divide the remainder of the page in half vertically with each of the two sections containing a boxed area or line to identify the following items. In other words, use two identical columns of this information.

- *Department, Class, Section*

4. Now divide each of the 2 vertical sections into 3 subcolumns with the following headings:

- *Exhibitor's Number, Award/Place, Premium Paid*

5. Provide an area at the bottom of the Premium Paid column to enter a total amount for the column. Use the heading, TOTAL PREMIUM PAID, to the left of where the total amount will appear.

PLAYER'S NOTES:

CLASS HOUR: ______ DATE: ______ NAME: ______________________

GAME 4— OVERTIME 1

Create a Label

PLAY TO EXECUTE

Design a label (sticker) that indicates a vehicle is eligible for reserved parking for the fairgrounds. The label should be easy to identify when displayed in the corner of the front window of any car entering the reserved parking section.

TACTICS TO INCLUDE

The following information should appear on the label. You decide on the dimensions of the label.

NAME OF FAIR: *Spring Harbor County Fair*

YEAR: *19—*

TYPE OF LABEL: *RESERVED PARKING*

GRAPHIC IMAGE: *Use the fair logo and a border of some kind.*

PLAYER'S NOTES:

CLASS HOUR: ______ DATE: ______ NAME: ____________________

GAME 4— OVERTIME 2

Create a Program

PLAY TO EXECUTE

Design a daily program to distribute at the fairgrounds entrance gates. The program should list the schedule of special activities happening throughout the day.

TACTICS TO INCLUDE

1. The following information should appear on the front side of the program. (This information is used daily.)

NAME OF FAIR: *Spring Harbor County Fair*

FORM TITLE: *Daily Program*

GRAPHIC IMAGE: *Use the fair logo.*

2. The following information should appear on the back side of the program. (This information will change daily.)

DATE OF PROGRAM: *Monday, August 13*

DAILY ACTIVITIES:

9:00 a.m.	*Rabbit Showmanship*
	Judging of Fruits & Vegetables
10:00 a.m.	*Kenneth V. Stover Farm Award Presentation (Horticulture Building)*
	Judging of Dairy
11:00 a.m.	*Youth Tractor Operators Challenge (South Parking Area)*
1:00 to 3:00 p.m.	*Sewing Demonstration (Home Economics Bldg.)*
2:00 p.m.	*Judging of Poultry*
	Handicapped Horseback Riding (Show Arena)
5:30 p.m.	*Parade with Trophy Winners for Monday*
6:30 p.m.	*TRACTOR PULL CONTEST (Grandstand)*

GRAPHIC IMAGE: *Use strawberry, chicken, or other appropriate images.*

PLAYER'S NOTES:

COACH'S CORNER

You did it! You won the championship on the last play of the game. Way to go—a perfect record (4-0). Several valuable experiences were gained during the season, and we hope you have discovered that desktop publishing certainly is a "game of inches." You managed to beat the strong defense of the competition by evaluating the situation and never losing sight of your overall goals to (1) use good techniques, (2) keep it simple, and (3) stay within your talents. And now for the final event of the *Publishing Season*, the *Sports Banquet*, where the coach will present the awards.

THE SPORTS BANQUET

Thanks for a great season! It has been rewarding work with you. Being a player on the DTP team has given you a brief introduction to the exciting world of desktop publishing. Hopefully it has inspired you to want to advance beyond the scope of DESKTOP PUBLISHING IN THE BAG. Remember that a true athlete must continue training to stay in top mental and physical shape.

And now the Coach will present you with your first DTP varsity letter for outstanding performance as a member of the team. Probably there were times when you wondered whether you would make it through the entire season. But you did—so congratulations!

Surprise! You were also voted MVP! What a way to end the season.

Hope to see you again next year.

GLOSSARY

A

Agenda A listing of the events that will occur or topics to discuss in a meeting.

Alignment How text appears in the column (flush left, flush right, centered, or justified).

Ascender The part of a character of type that extends above the letter. For example, the lowercase letter *h*.

B

Body Copy The main text in a document exclusive of headings.

Bold Type that is heavier in appearance than regular or normal type; also called *boldface*.

Border A line or frame surrounding graphics, graphs, illustrations, photographs, text, etc., that defines the edges. A border can be simple or elaborate.

Box Rule A line that has four sides to form a box; usually surrounds text or graphics.

Business Form A kind of document used to conduct daily business activities.

C

Camera-Ready The final copy of a publication used to produce the negative for a printing plate.

Caption Text used to describe an illustration or photograph; some captions are numbered.

Centering Aligning text evenly between the left and right margins.

Clip Art Ready-made graphic images (pictures, illustrations, symbols, etc.) saved to a file that can be retrieved and placed in a document. Clip-art files come in a variety of formats, depending on the software involved.

Clipboard A temporary holding area for the graphics or text that was last cut or copied in the layout.

Copy To duplicate a graphic image or text for placement in another location.

Crop To eliminate an unwanted area of a graphic image.

Cursor The blinking pointer on the screen indicating where the action will take place. The cursor can take on different shapes depending on the task being performed.

Cut To remove a graphic image or text from the present position on the page, thus allowing it to be moved elsewhere or deleted.

D

Default A value or setting used by your software program unless the program is instructed differently by the operator.

Descender The part of a character of type that descends below the letter. For example, the lowercase *g*.

Desktop Publishing The process of planning and creating computer-generated publications containing graphics and text that appear to have been professionally printed.

Dialog Box An area on the menu of a software package that asks for additional information needed to perform the desired command.

Dot-Matrix Printer An impact line printer; the images are printed by striking the paper with print pins through an inked ribbon.

Draft Quality The dry-run printing of a publication with a dot-matrix printer, not of reproduction quality; usually prints faster than higher quality methods.

Draw Program A software program that allows you to dreate the desired illustration to appear in a publication. This is also called a *paint program*.

Drop-Down Menu A software feature that provides a list of available choices within the selected menu-bar item. This is also called a *pull-down menu*.

DTP An abbreviation for desktop publishing.

DTP Text Editor The word processor in your desktop publishing software that allows you to work with text. This is also called a *word processor* or *story editor.*

E

Edit To make corrections and/or changes (add to or delete from) the existing text.

Element A unit (illustration/graphic or type/text) to be used in a publication.

F

Fill Pattern Various patterns from clear to opaque used to change the background of a defined shape. This is also called a *paint bucket* or *shades.*

Flip To turn the graphic image in the opposite direction horizontally or vertically.

Flush Left Aligning text with the left margin (also called *left-justified*).

Flush Right Aligning text with the right margin (also called *right-justified*).

Flyer A promotional poster used for various informational purposes.

Font A complete set of letters, numbers, and symbols in a single typeface and size.

Footer Text and a page number at the bottom of each page.

Frame An area on the screen of the DTP document that is created to hold and position text and/or graphic elements on the page.

G

Generic Book A book that is meant to be used with many different kinds of software.

Graphic An illustration created using a graphic software file, or a shape drawn with graphic tools.

Graphics Everything printed on the page except the words (text). Graphics consist of illustrations and design elements.

Graphic Tools DTP software features that add enhancements to your page layout.

Gutter The space between columns of text or inside margin for binding.

H

Hairline The thinnest line possible with your software; often used to define columns. Hairlines can be used as vertical or horizontal rules.

Hard Copy A printed copy of the page layout.

Header Text and a page number at the top of each page.

Headline Text in large type that calls attention to the body copy.

High-End Software Software with many features.

Highlighting To cause the text block to appear in reverse video, defining the area to be formatted or changed; also called *selecting* or *choosing an area or block.*

I

Icons Small symbolic pictures on the DTP software that show the tools that can be selected for working with text or graphics.

Italics A typeface variation that is slanted to the right.

J

Justified Aligning text with both the left and right margin even.

L

Landscape A page layout orientation that is wider than it is tall.

Laser Printer A printer that shows images transferred by laser beam on xerographic drum to paper, like a photocopier. This is usually a better quality printer than a dot-matrix printer.

Layout Arrangement of elements (graphics and text) on a page.

Leading The space between lines of type.

Letterhead The printed design on stationery that normally includes the name, address, and phone number. A logo may be included.

Live Area The space on the page layout between the margins where text and graphic elements are placed.

Logo A design created to identify or represent a specific company.

Low-End Software Software with few features.

M

Margins The white space at the top, sides, and bottom of a publication.

Masthead A consistent design that creates an identity for title, logo, and related information that appear on each issue of a newsletter.

Memorandum A form used for written communications between personnel in a business.

Menu Bar A list of the software program options available.

Monospace Typeface A typeface where all the characters are the same width.

Mouse A peripheral device that controls cursor movements on the screen of a computer.

N

Newsletter A form that is sent outside the business to clients on a regular basis to indicate company services and provide information.

O

On-Line Help A feature of the software that provides detailed information about performing a specific task.

P

Page Assembly Placing previously created text and graphic elements into a predefined page setup.

Page Layout Determining the placement of text and graphics on a page. This is also called *page composition.*

Page Setup The development of a page format that is often called a *blueprint.*

Page View The portion of a page that is displayed on the screen at one time. You can also see the entire page on the screen. Also called *zooming, showing a page, viewing a page, page mode, looking at the whole page,* or a *text mode window.*

Paste To anchor the graphic image or text in a new location; sometimes called stamping with graphic images.

Peripheral Devices Components that are external to the computer. For example, a printer and modem are peripheral devices.

Pica A unit of measurement commonly used in the printing industry. Six picas equals approximately one inch.

Point The smallest unit of measurement of type; 72 points equals one inch.

Portrait A page layout orientation that is taller than it is wide.

Printing Producing a hard copy of the completed page or pages.

Professional Statement A form used to bill a client for services rendered.

Pull Quote A short phrase or sentence pulled from an article, set in a larger size type than the body text.

R

Reproduction Quality High-quality printing of a publication done with a laser printer.

Resize To increase or decrease the size of a graphic image.

Resume A form used by an individual who is seeking a job. The form lists a person's background and qualifications for a career objective.

Reverse To switch to the opposite background display. If the background is black, change it to white and vice versa.

Rotate To turn the graphic image 90 degrees.

Rough A preliminary sketch to scale of where the elements will appear in a layout.

Rule A line of varying thickness from hairline to wide. You may be able to select the thickness of the rule with your software.

Ruler Guides Nonprinting horizontal and vertical measuring lines that can be used to position and/or align elements on the page layout.

S

Sans Serif A typeface without fine cross lines at the top and bottom of the main stroke of the characters.

Scanner An optical reading device that creates files that can be read by the computer.

Screen A pattern of dots from solid black to various levels of gray; screens are described in percentages, with 100% being solid black. A screen adds a tint to a defined area for special emphasis. This concept is similar to a fill pattern, only you do not have elaborate patterns—only patterns of dots. Also referred to as *shades*.

Scroll Bars Bars along the side of the screen used to quickly move the page horizontally or vertically to access a different part of the document.

Serif A typeface with a fine cross-line at the top and bottom of the main stroke of the characters.

Speciality Item Printed materials that are required by certain businesses or situations.

Spread A left- and right-hand page viewed together (two facing pages).

Style Sheet A file containing the type specifications and format information for a page design that can be used with different documents; also called *master pages*.

Subheads Headings that follow headlines for covering more detailed topics in the body copy.

T

Telephone Directory A listing of names and phone numbers of company personnel.

Template File A file on a diskette that stores the master version of a blank form. This file is then updated for different situations.

Text Words, numbers, and symbols that present information.

Text Block An identified section of text such as a word, a line, a sentence, a paragraph, a column, etc. This section of text has been highlighted.

Text Flow Text automatically continuing from the bottom of one column to the top of the next column.

Text Wrap Adjusting the appearance of text to follow the shape of an encountered graphic. The text formats around an illustration. This is also called *picturewrap* or *wrapping text*.

Thumbnail Sketch A rough version of the page design rendered in miniature.

Title Bar A feature of a software menu that displays the name of the file that is currently open.

Tool Box An area of the software screen that contains icons representing the tools that can be selected when working with text or graphics.

Trim Size The overall width and length of the paper on which your document is printed. A standard size is 8 1/2 inches by 11 inches.

Typeface A set of characters (letters, numbers, and symbols) that share the same design; sometimes erroneously called a *font*.

Type Size The measurement of the typeface; the distance between the top of the ascender and the bottom of the descender.

Type Style A variation in the enhancement of the typeface (e.g., boldface or italics).

W

White Space The area on a page where no text or graphic is placed.

Work Area The place on the screen where your layout of the document is done.

WYSIWYG The acronym for *What-You-See-Is-What-You-Get*.

PLANNING SHEET

THUMBNAIL SKETCH:

STYLE SPECIFICATIONS:

PAGE SIZE: ____________________ FILE NAME: ____________________

MARGINS — TOP: __________ BOTTOM: __________ SIDES: __________

NUMBER OF COLUMNS: __________ SIZE: __________ GUTTER SIZE: __________

TEXT (typeface, style, size):

GRAPHICS (images, charts, illustrations):

ENHANCEMENTS (lines, boxes, borders, screens):

PLANNING SHEET

THUMBNAIL SKETCH:

STYLE SPECIFICATIONS:

PAGE SIZE: ____________________ FILE NAME: ____________________

MARGINS — TOP: ____________ BOTTOM: ____________ SIDES: ____________

NUMBER OF COLUMNS: ________ SIZE: ____________________ GUTTER SIZE: ____________

TEXT (typeface, style, size):

GRAPHICS (images, charts, illustrations):

ENHANCEMENTS (lines, boxes, borders, screens):

PLANNING SHEET

THUMBNAIL SKETCH:

STYLE SPECIFICATIONS:

PAGE SIZE: ______________________ **FILE NAME:** ______________________

MARGINS — TOP: ______________ **BOTTOM:** ______________ **SIDES:** ______________

NUMBER OF COLUMNS: __________ **SIZE:** ______________________ **GUTTER SIZE:** ______________

TEXT (typeface, style, size):

GRAPHICS (images, charts, illustrations):

ENHANCEMENTS (lines, boxes, borders, screens):

PLANNING SHEET

THUMBNAIL SKETCH:

STYLE SPECIFICATIONS:

PAGE SIZE: ____________________ **FILE NAME:** ____________________

MARGINS — TOP: ______________ **BOTTOM:** ______________ **SIDES:** ______________

NUMBER OF COLUMNS: __________ **SIZE:** ____________________ **GUTTER SIZE:** __________

TEXT (typeface, style, size):

GRAPHICS (images, charts, illustrations):

ENHANCEMENTS (lines, boxes, borders, screens):

PLANNING SHEET

THUMBNAIL SKETCH:

STYLE SPECIFICATIONS:

PAGE SIZE: ______________________ FILE NAME: ______________________________

MARGINS — TOP: _______________ BOTTOM: _______________ SIDES: _____________________________

NUMBER OF COLUMNS: __________ SIZE: _________________________ GUTTER SIZE: ______________

TEXT (typeface, style, size):

GRAPHICS (images, charts, illustrations):

ENHANCEMENTS (lines, boxes, borders, screens):

PLANNING SHEET

THUMBNAIL SKETCH:

STYLE SPECIFICATIONS:

PAGE SIZE: ____________________ **FILE NAME:** ____________________

MARGINS — TOP: ____________ **BOTTOM:** ____________ **SIDES:** ____________________

NUMBER OF COLUMNS: __________ **SIZE:** ____________________ **GUTTER SIZE:** ____________

TEXT (typeface, style, size):

GRAPHICS (images, charts, illustrations):

ENHANCEMENTS (lines, boxes, borders, screens):

PLANNING SHEET

THUMBNAIL SKETCH:

STYLE SPECIFICATIONS:

PAGE SIZE: ______________________ **FILE NAME:** ______________________________

MARGINS — TOP: _______________ **BOTTOM:** _______________ **SIDES:** ______________________

NUMBER OF COLUMNS: __________ **SIZE:** ________________________ **GUTTER SIZE:** _______________

TEXT (typeface, style, size):

GRAPHICS (images, charts, illustrations):

ENHANCEMENTS (lines, boxes, borders, screens):

PLANNING SHEET

THUMBNAIL SKETCH:

STYLE SPECIFICATIONS:

PAGE SIZE: ______________________ **FILE NAME:** ______________________________

MARGINS — TOP: _______________ **BOTTOM:** _______________ **SIDES:** _____________________

NUMBER OF COLUMNS: ___________ **SIZE:** ________________________ **GUTTER SIZE:** _______________

TEXT (typeface, style, size):

GRAPHICS (images, charts, illustrations):

ENHANCEMENTS (lines, boxes, borders, screens):

PLANNING SHEET

THUMBNAIL SKETCH:

STYLE SPECIFICATIONS:

PAGE SIZE: ______________________ FILE NAME: ______________________________

MARGINS — TOP: ______________ BOTTOM: ______________ SIDES: ____________________________

NUMBER OF COLUMNS: __________ SIZE: ________________________ GUTTER SIZE: _______________

TEXT (typeface, style, size):

GRAPHICS (images, charts, illustrations):

ENHANCEMENTS (lines, boxes, borders, screens):

CONGRATULATIONS!

____

has made the DPT team for demonstrating outstanding desktop publishing skills!

Desktop Publishing in the Bag

South-Western Publishing Co.

____
The Coach

____
Date